French Braid Quilts

with a twist

New Variations for Vibrant Strip-Pieced Projects

Jane Hardy Miller

C&T PUBLISHING

Publisher: Amy Marson

Creative Director: Gailen Runge

Art Director: Kristy Zacharias

Editor: Liz Aneloski

Technical Editors: Carolyn Aune and Teresa Stroin

Cover Designers: Kristen Yenche and April Mostek

Book Designer: Kristen Yenche

Production Coordinator: Jenny Davis

Production Editor: Joanna Burgarino

Illustrator: Tim Manibusan

Photo Assistant: Mary Peyton Peppo

Instructional photography by Diane Pedersen, unless otherwise noted

Published by C&T Publishing, Inc., P.O. Box 1456, Lafayette, CA 94549

Library of Congress Cataloging-in-Publication Data

Miller, Jane Hardy, 1950-

French braid quilts with a twist : new variations for vibrant strip-pieced projects / Jane Hardy Miller.

   pages cm

ISBN 978-1-60705-882-3 (soft cover)

1. Strip quilting--Patterns. I. Title.

TT835.M51525 2014

746.46--dc23

                                    2013049472

Printed in China

10 9 8 7 6 5 4 3 2 1

Contents

DEDICATION & ACKNOWLEDGMENTS ...4

INTRODUCTION...5

WHAT YOU NEED TO KNOW...6

Equipment...6

Fabric Selection...8

French Braid Construction...8

Piecing Basic Braids...8

Piecing Center-Out Braids...10

Adding Ending Triangles...11

Marking and Trimming...12

Separators...16

Nonbraid Columns...17

Borders...18

Invisible (from the Front) Machine Binding...19

PROJECTS

Double-Accent French Braid ...22

Variable-Length French Braid ...27

Scrappy French Braid ...34

Variable-Width French Braid ...40

French Braid Stars ...45

Crazy Braid ...55

Parquet ...61

Triplex ...68

ABOUT THE AUTHOR...79

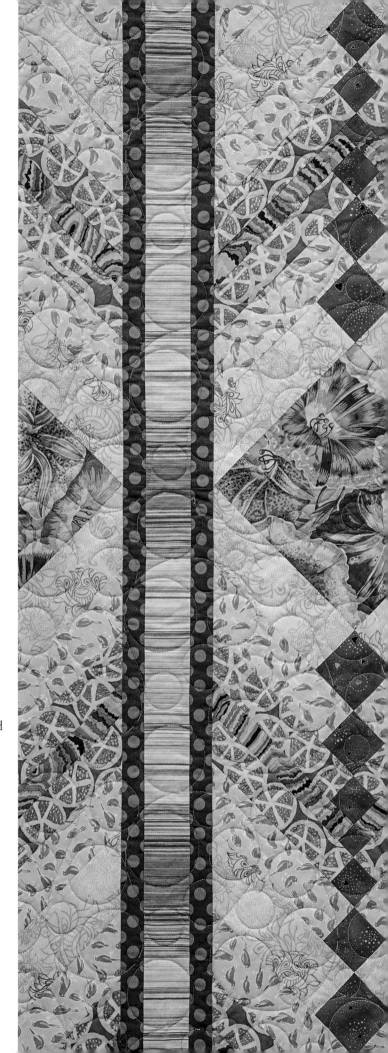

Dedication

This book is dedicated to quilt shop owners everywhere. They help us choose our projects, pick our fabrics, and befriend our sewing machines. Where would we be without them?

Acknowledgments

Writing an instructional book about quilting really is a group effort. There are a few obvious helpers: quilters Patricia E. Ritter, Marybeth O'Halloran, and Heather Spence, all of whom graciously shoehorned my work into their busy schedules. Less obvious are a group of quilters in Miami (they know who they are), who are willing to try almost any pattern before it's published; Chrissy O'Connor, who graciously tested the binding instructions; and Joan Bailey McMath, who is still the best proofreader I know. Anything that works well in this book is because of them, and anything that doesn't probably wasn't seen by them. My editors, Liz Aneloski and Carolyn Aune, played a huge part, as did the book designer, Kristen Yenche, and others at C&T Publishing whose names I don't even know. Least apparent of all are the students, co-workers, and family members whose interest and encouragement over the years have motivated me to become a better quilter. In the end it's all about time on the clock. And obsession.

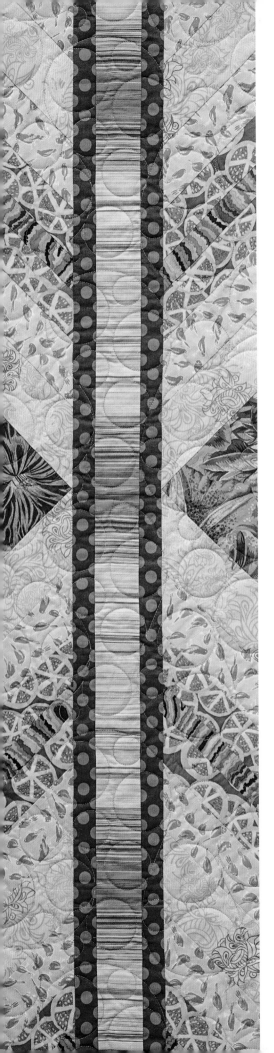

Introduction

During the approximately eleven years that I've been making French Braid quilts, the same two questions have arisen repeatedly. This book was written in part to address them.

The first issue is the twelve-fabric braid run, the fabrics that appear as chevrons in the braids. Because they are the most noticeable aspect of the braids, they set the tone for the finished quilt. I have always been a proponent of a twelve-fabric closely shaded braid run. But as I saw more French Braids over the years, I realized that even those with less-than-perfect braid runs still looked good. I tried using fewer fabrics in the braid run and repeating them more often. Eventually the success of those projects (pages 27 and 40) made me wonder whether a less organized type of French Braid could still be attractive (yes), and whether it would be any easier to select fabric for one (also yes). Since I've always loved scrap quilts, it was only a short time until I tried a French Braid version (page 34).

Second, if you are among the many quilters who have asked whether the size of the segments could be changed, this book is for you. The segment sizes vary, not only from quilt to quilt but within some of the quilts. In fact, if you're brave enough to try it, there's even one in which the segments aren't even rectangles.

So, I'm still careful in selecting a braid run, perhaps more so than most quilters. But in this book, I've tried to make choosing the fabrics easier. The braid runs have been simplified by using fewer fabrics, as well as by placing less emphasis on perfection in the braid run, and the quilts use many sizes of segments. I hope this evolving style will encourage quilters who have previously been intimidated by French Braids to try one.

What You Need to Know

Equipment

You probably already own most of the equipment needed to make any quilt in this book: a sewing machine with a reliable straight stitch and a ¼″ foot, and basic sewing supplies such as pins and scissors. The structural integrity of your quilt depends on the thread; save the 10-spools-for-$1 for another project and get out the good stuff. The same is true of your fabric: you'll put a lot of time into making a quilt, so don't devalue your effort by using an inferior product.

All the projects in this book include strip piecing, so you will also need a rotary cutter, mat, and, depending on the project, at least one long, wide ruler—6″ × 24″ or even 8½″ × 24″. I also often use a shorter ruler (4″ × 14″) for cutting segments, and the nonbraid projects may require an additional large square ruler and a second long, wide ruler. Please remember that a rotary cutter is a dangerous implement; the best way to avoid injury is to pay attention while using it.

You will need a sharp pencil for marking the sides of the braids or columns. A mechanical pencil works best, as the marked line is always the same width. Failing that, have a pencil sharpener available while you mark. It is theoretically possible to mark in ink, since you're marking the cutting line rather than the sewing line. But in case of error, ink is harder to remove than pencil, and ink can shadow through or bleed onto other fabrics.

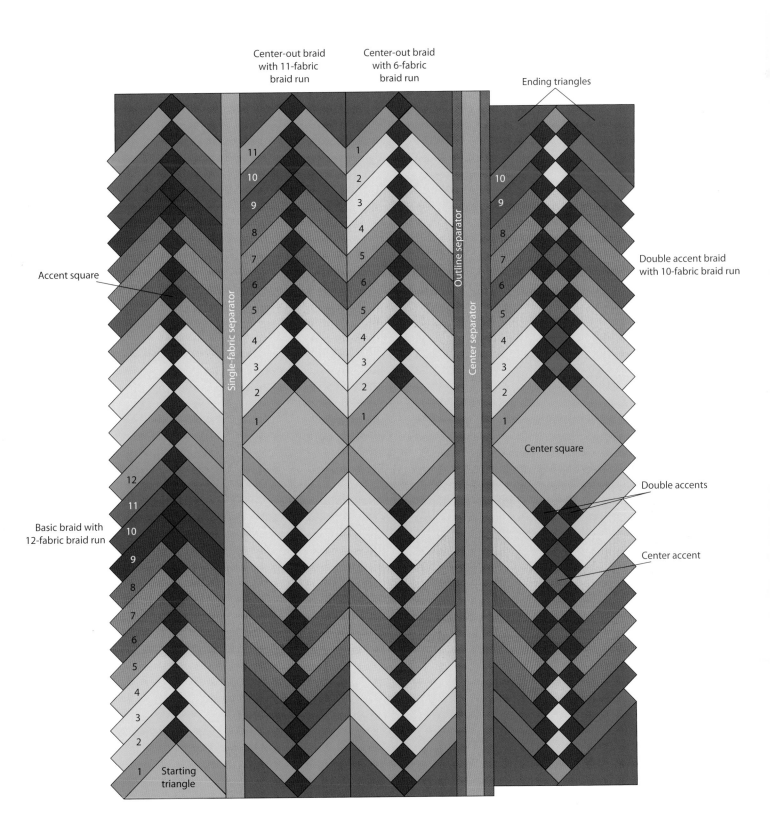

Center-out braid with 11-fabric braid run

Center-out braid with 6-fabric braid run

Ending triangles

Accent square

Single-fabric separator

Outline separator

Center separator

Double accent braid with 10-fabric braid run

Basic braid with 12-fabric braid run

Center square

Double accents

Center accent

Starting triangle

Fabric Selection

Fabric selection for the French Braid projects varies with the number of fabrics in the braid run, and more specific fabric suggestions are given with some of the projects. However, there are a few constants. Try to make the braid run flow—it doesn't have to be perfect, but it's nice if there isn't a large jump. And no matter how great the fabrics look at the store or on your cutting mat, the braid will look very different when it's sewn; because of this, try to purchase the ending triangle, separator, and border fabrics after the braids are completed.

There are a few scrappy French Braids in this book (*It's Easy Being Green*, page 34; *Fruit of the Vine*, page 39; and *Black and Gray and Red All Over*, page 39), and fabric selection for those is more forgiving—almost anything goes. However, there are a few pitfalls to avoid. Do not use diagonally patterned prints in the braid run, because the print will run vertically on one side of the braid and horizontally on the other. Large, high-contrast prints can sometimes appear as blotches in the braid run; unfortunately, there's no way to tell in advance whether this will add interest or merely be distracting. Be careful of stripes that run parallel to the selvages, because they often create a visual stopping point in the braids. Stripes that run perpendicular to the selvages seem to have less of this effect but can still be unpredictable.

For starting or ending triangles, avoid regular geometric prints such as stripes and plaids, or any motif that appears in straight lines or rows; the ends of the braids are not always perfectly square, and straight lines will often be askew. Directional motifs or one-way designs will work for the starting triangles or center squares as long as you understand that you may need to allow extra fabric for fussy cutting. However, use of a directional print for ending triangles may require cutting each triangle individually.

French Braid Construction

This book features two types of French Braids: basic braids and center-out braids. Each will be discussed separately. Although your segments may be proportioned differently than those in the illustrations in those sections, the technique is always the same.

I don't usually pin as I add the segments, but if you can't match the top ends and seams without pinning, do so. I also strongly suggest that you lay out one entire braid run with the center square or starting triangle before beginning to sew. This will give you a chance to change or rearrange the braid fabrics before the braid is sewn together.

PIECING BASIC BRAIDS

1. Follow the instructions for your project to cut the required number and size of segments and the starting triangles.

2. Lay a starting triangle on the table in front of you, with the 90° corner pointing away from you.

3. Select an unaccented segment of braid fabric #1, which is usually shorter than the triangle side. Place the segment right sides together on the left side of the triangle. Align the long edge with the side of the triangle and the top of the segment with the top corner of the triangle.

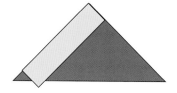

Align segment with side of triangle and top corner.

4. Rotate the triangle and sew from the unaligned end of the segment to the top of the triangle, as shown. Although this is counterintuitive, always sew with the newest segment on top as you feed it into the machine. This will help ensure that the finished braids are the same length on both long sides. Repeat this process with the remaining triangles, chaining them if possible.

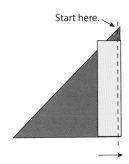

Sew from unaligned end of segment.

5. Cut the triangles apart. Press the seams away from the starting triangle every time you add a set of segments. Finger-pressing does not work well; use an iron.

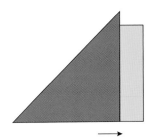

Press seams away from triangle.

6. Lay a triangle on the table in front of you again, orienting it in the original position. Select an accented segment of braid fabric #1. Lay it on the top right edge of the triangle.

7. Match the long sides, the edges at the top corner, and the seams. Start sewing at the accent end of the segment. Repeat this process with the remaining triangles, chaining them if possible.

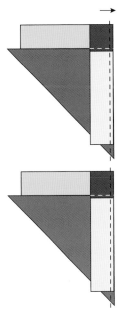

Match corners and seams, and start sewing at accent end.

8. Cut the triangles apart. Press all the seams away from the starting triangle. If you decide to omit the separators in any project, press all the seams on this side of the braid toward the starting triangle.

9. Continue adding braid segments as in Steps 4–8, following the order given in your chosen pattern.

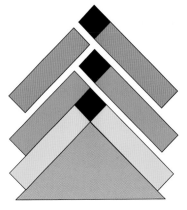

Continue adding segments.

PIECING CENTER-OUT BRAIDS

This process is similar to the basic braid. The only difference is that segments are added to two opposite sides of a square rather than to one side of a triangle.

1. Follow the instructions for your project to cut the required number and size of segments and the center squares.

2. Lay a center square on the table in front of you, with a corner pointing toward you. That corner will be either a top or a bottom corner in the finished quilt, so orient directional fabric accordingly.

3. Select an unaccented segment of braid fabric #1, which is longer than the center square. Place the segment on the top left side of the square. Align a long edge on the side of the square and the top of the segment with the top corner of the center square.

Place segment on top left of square.

4. Rotate the square and sew from the unaligned end of the segment to the top of the square as shown. Repeat this process with the remaining center squares, chaining them if possible.

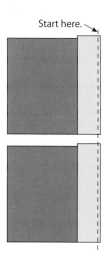

Start here.

Sew starting at unaligned edge of segment.

5. Cut the squares apart, turn them 180°, and repeat the process on the opposite side of each center square. Press the seams away from the center square every time you add a set of segments. Finger-pressing does not work well; use an iron.

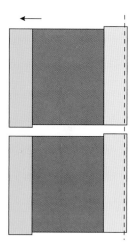

Repeat on opposite side of square. Press using iron.

6. Lay a center square on the table in front of you again, orienting it in the original direction. If your center square fabric is directional and the print is either right side up or upside down, you have sewn correctly. If the directional print is lying on its side, take off the segments, reorient the center square, and resew the segments (Steps 2–5).

7. Select an accented segment of braid fabric #1. Lay it on the top right edge of the center square.

8. Match the long sides, the edges at the top corner, and the seams. Start sewing at the accent end of the segment. Repeat this process with the remaining center squares, chaining them if possible.

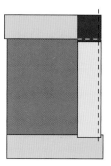

Align top corner and seams and sew.

9. Cut the squares apart, turn them 180°, and repeat the process on the opposite edge of each center square. Press all the seams away from the center square. If you decide to omit the separators in any project, press all the seams on this side of the braid toward the center square.

10. Continue adding braid segments as in Steps 3–9, following the order given in the instructions for your chosen pattern, until you have finished adding segments.

ADDING ENDING TRIANGLES

1. When you have used all the braid segments, add an ending triangle to the left side of the end of each braid (on both left ends for center-out braids), matching the long edges. Leave a bit more than usual of the triangle (about ¾″) hanging off the top edge of the braid. Pin the triangle to the braid. Flip it over so the bias edge of the triangle is underneath the braid as it goes through the machine; sew. Press the seam toward the triangle.

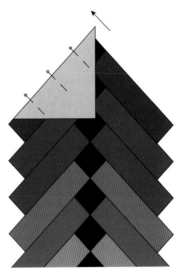

Pin and then flip over to sew with triangle under braid.

2. Add an ending triangle to the right side of the end of each braid, again matching the long edges. This time the *top of the seamline* on the long edge of the new triangle should meet the top raw edge of the triangle you just added; there will be about ⅜″ hanging off the top edge. Pin, flip the braid over, and sew as before. Press the seam toward the triangles.

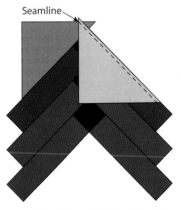

Add triangle to right side of braid.

MARKING AND TRIMMING

Marking the sides of the braids is undoubtedly the most tedious step in the process of making a French Braid. However, if you take care here you will experience benefits later when adding the separators, and you will be surprised at how quickly your marking skills improve as you go.

The sides of the braids are now zigzags. To sew them to separators, you must mark a straight line that will ultimately be the cutting line. There are three goals in this process: marking the sides, trimming the ends, and measuring the length of each braid. You will need a rotary cutter and mat, a wide ruler, and a pencil in a color that will be visible on all your fabrics. Mechanical pencils work best here, because they make a thin line and stay sharp; if you use another type, keep a sharpener handy to avoid wide lines that make it difficult to know where to align the separators later.

1. Press each center-out braid carefully by starting at the center and pressing in one direction at a time. If you are pressing a basic braid, begin at a starting triangle and press the entire length of the braid. In either case, gently press left and right in a sweeping motion as you work your way toward the end of the braid. Your aim is to make sure that all the seam allowances and any pleats in the seams are pressed flat, all without stretching the braid. Try not to let the braid hang off the ironing board.

2. Take the braid to a cutting mat, which will help stabilize it for marking as well as for cutting. Starting with an ending-triangle end of the braid, lay out as much as possible in the available space and accordion-fold it at the other end. The unfolded end of the braid should be near the end of the mat. Do not let either end hang off the edge of the table. Align the outer points of one side of the braid with a line on the mat. The longer the braid is, the more flexible it will be, so take care in the alignment.

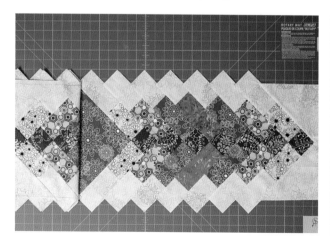

Lay out braid on mat.

Align points with line on mat.

3. Use the centermost accent points (the braid's midline) as a reference point and measure out to the innermost point where there is still fabric—the inner corner at the end of a segment. Do this in a few places and on both sides of the braid. You're trying to decide how far out you can eventually cut. This will be the cutting line, not the sewing line, so don't worry if there are a couple of threads missing from under the very edge of the ruler.

When you have a good estimate (5¾″, for example), lay the corresponding line of the ruler (the 5¾″ line) on the midline of the braid and recheck to see whether you will be able to catch all the edges when marking. Look at the outer edge of the ruler to see where the cut edge of the braid will eventually be. If the edge of the ruler falls too far off the edge of the braid to catch the inner corners in the seam, move the ruler closer to the midline of the braid.

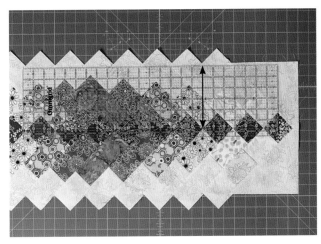

Measure from center of braid to innermost point.

4. Once you have determined the width, start at the end of the braid and place the selected line of the ruler on the braid's midline. Mark the edge with a pencil. Mark as much of the braid as you can without unfolding it. Without moving the braid, repeat the process on the opposite long edge. Then complete Step 5 on this first end.

Mark line.

5. Trim the excess fabric off the ending triangle end of the braid by placing the ¼" line of your ruler exactly at the top point of the top accent square. On each side of the braid, align a ruler line with the pencil marks you just drew. Recheck the ¼" line at the top and realign the ruler if necessary. When you're sure that the ruler is perpendicular to the drawn lines and that the ¼" line is on the accent point, cut. Trim only the end at this point, *not* the sides of the braid.

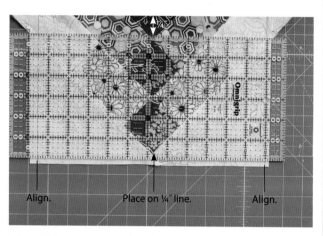

Place ¼" line on accent point and trim excess ending-triangle fabric.

6. Move the marked and trimmed section of the braid off the mat, accordion-fold it if necessary, and unfold the next section. Align the edge of the braid as before. For a center-out braid, lay the ruler down on the length of the braid to see whether your next set of marks will reach the center square. If so, place the ¼" line of your ruler on the outermost point of the center square, or its frame if your project calls for one, align the other end of the ruler with the end of the line you just drew, and draw a new line.

IMPORTANT

If your ruler doesn't yet reach the center square, unfold the braid so that the area around the center square can be marked next. Place one end of the ruler as directed in Step 6; align the other end with the accents as directed in Step 4. Draw a line; repeat the process for the other side. Then connect the end of that line with the one you drew on the end of the braid. Measure across the center square from line to line and compare that number with the width of the braid near the previously marked end. A small difference (⅛") is acceptable. If the difference is larger than that, you will have to move your marked line and, depending on the placement, either cut off the points of the center square or float it on the background when you sew.

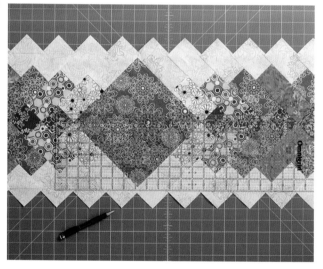

Continue to draw line.

7. Continue realigning and marking the braid until the entire length is marked. When you get to the other end of a center-out braid, trim as directed in Step 5.

If you have made a basic braid, you must also trim the starting triangle end of the braid. Cut from the point where your drawn line intersects the seam attaching the first segment to the triangle, to the same point on the other edge of the braid. This cutting line is not always parallel to the bottom of the starting triangle.

Cut where drawn line intersects seam.

Trim starting triangle.

IMPORTANT

If the first segment seam doesn't extend all the way to the drawn line, draw an imaginary line lengthening the seamline until it meets the pencil line.

8. Measure the braid down the center from end to end without stretching it; write the number down. Do this for every braid, as the lengths will probably not all be the same. It may be more convenient to fold the braid in half, wrong sides together, match the center tops at the ends, and measure down the center of the braid. If you do this, match the ends at the top points of the top accent square even if that means that the braid ends are uneven near the sides. Then use the half-length number when cutting folded separators and borders. If this system seems too confusing, ignore it and use your usual method to measure the lengths.

SEPARATORS

Separators add width to the quilt and frame the braids. More importantly, they stabilize the quilt top and ensure that all the braids are the same length in the finished top. Because the braids are on the bias, it is important to use the lengthwise grain, which is the most stable, for the separators. This is especially beneficial for longer braids. You may occasionally deviate from this rule for either design reasons or lack of fabric, but try to use the lengthwise grain, even if it takes more fabric or means that there are more seams in the separators.

1. First determine a universal length for the braids and separators. Look at the numbers you wrote down in Step 8 (page 15)—there is probably a range of about ½″ to ¾″. Choose a number that's somewhere in the middle but still easy to deal with. For example, if the lengths of your 3 braids are 57½″, 57⅞″, and 58⅛″, you might pick 57¾″ as the universal length, even though it's neither the length of any of the braids nor their average.

> ### tip
>
> The width of the separators in the individual patterns is always based on their appearance. If your separators look better wider or narrower than instructed in the pattern, change them.

2. Check the project instructions to see how many separators you need, usually 1 less than the number of braids. Construct the required number, each 1″–2″ longer than the braids. Then trim them to the universal length.

❖ If you are making a 1-fabric separator, sew pieces end to end to obtain the required length.

❖ If you are making a 2-fabric separator, sew pieces of each fabric end to end before piecing the 3 parts (outline separator, center separator, outline separator) together.

❖ If you are making a pieced separator, sew the pieces of the center separator together as directed before adding the outline separators.

Press the seams. If one of the separator fabrics is much darker than the other, press the seams toward the darker fabric. Otherwise, press them toward the center separator. Mark the center of each long side of each separator.

3. Mark the center on each side of each braid.

❖ If you are working with a center-out braid, the centers are the outer side corners of the center square.

❖ If you are working with a basic braid, find the centers by first folding the braid in half crosswise and placing a pin at the fold on the pencil line on each side of each braid. When you look at all the pins you will see that some will be farther away from the nearest seam than others. Pick a point closer than the farthest pin from the pencil line / seam intersection and farther than the closest—in essence, you're averaging the distances so the centers of the braids will be at the same point on both sides of all the braids. When you have determined the center point—say, ¼″ up the pencil line from a specific seam—make a mark on the pencil lines at the same point on both sides of each braid. This will ensure that the chevrons of the braids will be aligned across the width of the quilt.

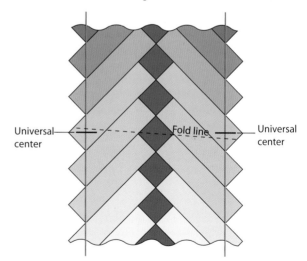

Determining center of basic braid

4. Lay out a braid faceup on a table. If necessary, accordion-fold the end you're not working on; do not let the end hang off the edge of the table. Place a separator facedown on top of the braid. Align the long raw edge of the separator with one of the marked lines on the braid. Match and pin the centers and ends, and then pin at every seam between the first pins. Repeat this process for every separator/braid pair. If the direction of the center squares is important, be sure to sew all the separators to the same—left or right—side of each column.

> **tip**
>
> If you must stretch or compress the braid a lot, you have probably erred in measuring or cutting the separators. Stop and remeasure everything before continuing.

Align long edge of separator strip on marked line on braid.

5. Use the edge of the separator as a guide for the edge of your ¼″ foot and sew the seam. Sew at a moderate speed, as the foot has a tendency to jump off the seamline as it crosses the diagonal seams.

6. Use a long ruler and your rotary cutter to trim off the jagged braid edge that extends beyond the raw edge of the separator. Press the seam toward the separator.

> **CAUTION:** Make sure that other sections of the braid are not lying under the area you're trimming.

Trim off excess braid.

7. Repeat Steps 4–6 to sew the braids into pairs, using the same techniques. Then sew together the pairs and any odd braids to create the quilt top.

8. If you will be adding the side borders first, cut them the universal length. If you will be adding the top and bottom borders first, use the universal length plus twice the *finished* width of the top and bottom borders as the length of the first side borders.

Nonbraid Columns

The nonbraid patterns in the book are made without separators, although you could easily add them by following the instructions in Separators (page 16). Because the columns are sewn directly to each other, their preparation is slightly different. Instead of marking the edges, you will cut them off and trim the ends of each column before sewing it to its neighbor. Since the treatment of the columns differs slightly, specific instructions are given with each pattern.

Borders

Borders define and frame your quilt, so select an inner border fabric that will contrast with the fabrics in the quilt top as well as with the outer border or borders. For French Braid quilts, the outline separator fabric can sometimes double as an inner border.

These instructions are for a quilt with two sets of borders, inner and outer, which is the case for most of the quilts in this book. When using this method, add the end inner borders first if you are adding an even number of border sets (inner and outer borders). Add the side borders first if you are adding an odd number of border sets (inner, second, and outer). No matter how many sets of borders you add, the process remains the same.

Instructions in some steps differ slightly for French Braid and non–French Braid quilts, such as *Parquet* (page 61) and *Triplex* (page 68). Read carefully to ensure that the border instructions apply to your project.

1. If you have not cut the borders as 1 piece, sew the pieces end to end to obtain enough length. Press the seams open.

2. Measure across the center of the quilt.

❖ **French Braid quilt:** Measure across the center from pencil line to pencil line. Cut 2 end inner borders that length.

❖ **Non–French Braid quilt:** Measure across the center from edge to edge. Cut 2 end inner borders that length.

3. Pin 1 end border to each end of the quilt top, sew, and press the seams toward the borders.

❖ **French Braid quilt:** Match the center of the top to the center of the border, and the ends of the borders to the pencil lines on each side of the top.

❖ **Non–French Braid quilt:** Match the centers and ends.

4. Measure the length of the quilt down the center.

❖ **French Braid quilt:** This number should equal the universal length plus twice the *finished* width of the inner border. For example, if the universal length is 60″ and the inner borders are cut 1½″, this number would be 62″. Write the number down, as it will eventually be the final cut side border length you use in Step 6. Then add about 1½″ to allow for any reduction in the border length when you sew the strips together. Cut 2 inner border strips and 2 outer border strips, each this length. In the above example that would be 63½″ (62″ plus 1½″ for insurance).

❖ **Non–French Braid quilt:** Start by measuring the length of the top including the borders you just added; write down the number. Then add an extra 1½″ and cut 2 side inner and 2 side outer border strips that length.

5. Sew a side inner border strip to each side outer border strip, being sure to make both left and right borders if you are using directional fabric. Press the seams toward the outer borders.

6. Cut each side border.

❖ **French Braid quilt:** Cut each side border pair down to the original length you wrote down in Step 4. Pin 1 set to each side of the quilt, matching the ends and centers. Sew. Press the seams toward the borders.

❖ **Non–French Braid quilt:** Cut each side border pair down to the length you wrote down in Step 4. Pin 1 set to each side of the quilt, matching the ends and centers. Sew. Press the seams toward the borders.

7. Measure across the center of the quilt to find the new width. Cut 2 outer border strips that length. Pin 1 to each end of the quilt, matching the ends and centers of the borders to the sides and center of the quilt. Pay attention to the orientation of the borders if you are using a directional fabric. Sew. Press the seams toward the outer borders. (Had you been adding a third set of borders, you would have sewn the second and third borders together before adding them to the ends, and so forth.)

Invisible (from the Front) Machine Binding

Some quilters enjoy the handwork involved in whipping their bindings down to the backs of their quilts; I'm not one of them. But because I also don't like seeing obvious stitching in the binding on the front of the quilt, I developed a method of sewing the binding entirely by machine in a way that looks from the front as if the back had been whipped down by hand. You will need strong pins and a walking foot for this method, and a quilting glove for your left hand is very helpful. It will probably take several tries before you are successful, especially at the corners. But if, like me, you are highly motivated to find an aesthetically acceptable, faster way to bind your quilts, you will persist and eventually master it. In the photos at the right, the front of the quilt is the tone-on-tone blue fabric and the back is the busy blue and pink. The instructions show mitered corners for the binding, but this technique will also work for rounded corners.

1. Set the stitch length as you usually do for binding. If you have a needle-down function on your machine, engage it. If not, use the handwheel to sink the needle into the quilt every time you stop.

2. Make continuous bias binding or cut either bias or straight strips ¼″ wider than usual. Sew the long strips together end to end and press the wrong sides together along the length. At this point the strip will be ⅛″ wider than your usual binding.

3. Thread your machine, top and bobbin, with thread that matches the binding as closely as possible. (Yellow thread was used in the photos to make the stitching more visible.)

4. Attach the walking foot to your machine and sew the binding to the front of the quilt. Start sewing in the middle of an edge. When you come to a corner, fold and turn the binding as you would for any binding. When the sewing is complete, connect the 2 ends of the binding with a seam. When you get a bit better at the invisible machine binding technique, you will probably want to take a slightly (a few threads) deeper seam, but just sew as usual for the first few times.

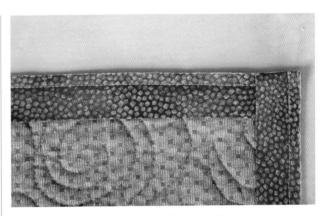
Sew binding to front of quilt.

5. Starting in the middle of a long straight stretch of binding, turn a few inches of the folded edge of the binding to the back of the quilt, making sure that the fold covers the original stitching. Secure the loose folded edge of the binding by pinning in the ditch from the front of the quilt, parallel to the edge.

Bring binding to back and pin in ditch on front of quilt.

Pins through folded binding on back of quilt.

6. Continue pinning in this manner, with the pins as close together as possible. When you get to the corner where the binding has been mitered, fold it around to the back as before. This time place the point of a pin very close to, but not at, the spot where the binding seam turns the corner. The pin should enter the fabric about ⅛″ away from the corner and come up about ½″ away. If there is space between the corner pin and the pin you placed before that, add another pin between them.

Fold first fold of mitered corner and pin.

7. Fold the adjacent side of the binding to the back, forming a miter as you do. You may have to play with it a bit to make the 2 edges meet at the back corner.

Fold second fold of mitered corner.

8. Pin this second side of the corner down, making sure that the point of the pin comes up exactly in the corner of the seamline.

Pin second fold.   Back of pinned corner

9. Continue pinning until you have pinned all 4 sides. If you run out of pins before you finish, sew as directed below until you are about 8″ from the last pin. Use the pins you've removed to continue pinning. This can be done while the quilt remains in the machine, but if you decide to remove it, take a couple of backstitches first.

10. Rethread your machine with a top thread that matches the quilt's border fabric and a bobbin thread that matches the binding. If either of these fabrics is a color that is difficult to match, or a multicolor print, consider substituting invisible nylon thread. (For ease of visibility, black thread was used on both sides in the photos.)

11. If you haven't pinned all the way around the quilt yet, go to the first and second pins you placed. If you have pinned all the way around, start with any 2 pins in a long straight stretch. Push the first pin (with the yellow head in the photo) further into the fabric, as far as it will easily go. Pull the second pin (with the white head in the photo) out so that the point barely remains in the fabric.

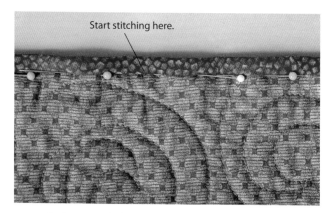

Push one pin (yellow head) all the way into the fabric.
Pull a second pin (white head) out so the point barely remains in the fabric.

12. Slide the edge of the quilt under the walking foot in the space between the 2 pins. Use the handwheel to lower the needle exactly into the ditch between the border and the binding, about ½″ from the point of the second pin. Backstitch 2 or 3 stitches.

13. Grasp the head of the second pin with the thumb and forefinger of your right hand and rest the side of your hand on the bed of the machine. If you keep your hand in the same place while you slowly sew forward in the ditch, the movement of the quilt forward through the machine will cause the pin to come out of the fabric by itself. Leave the first pin where it is.

Grasp pin and slowly sew forward.

14. Use your left hand to guide and control the quilt as you continue in this manner. When you approach the first corner, your goal is for the needle to come down exactly where the binding seam turns the corner. Before you get to that point, pull out the pin on the adjacent side until the point barely remains in the fabric. Shorten your stitch length for the last 1 or 2 stitches if necessary and pull only the point of the pin out of the way before you take the final stitch. Leave the needle down in the quilt.

Insert needle exactly where binding seam turns corner.

15. Lift the walking foot and turn the quilt. Continue sewing and removing pins in the same manner until you have sewn around the entire perimeter back to the first pin. Backstitch 1 or 2 stitches and remove the quilt from the machine.

Front of stitched binding

Back of stitched binding

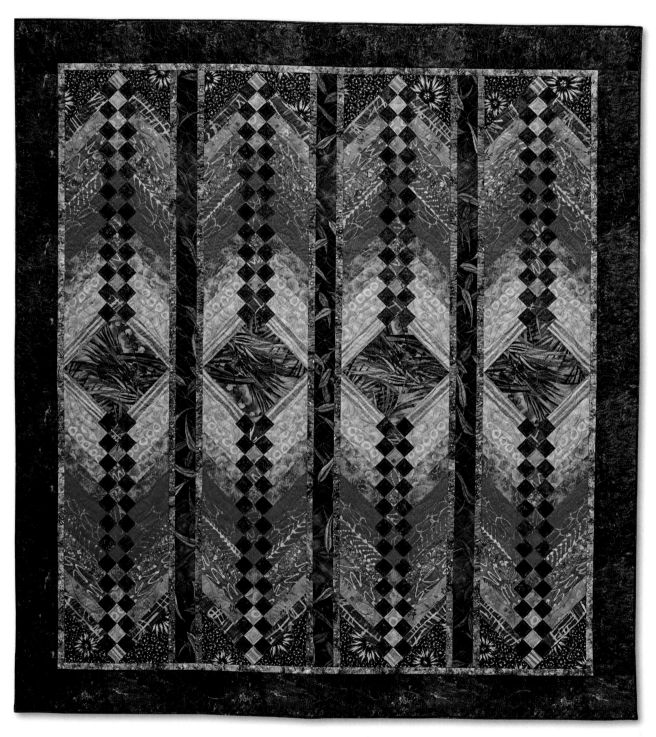

Jungle Braid, 90˝ × 97˝ ❖ quilted by Marybeth O'Halloran

Select the braid fabrics first, shading from color to color in groups, referring to the project quilt photo. Select accent and center square fabrics to go with the braid run and purchase the other fabrics after the braids are completed. Braid fabrics are numbered 1 through 12, counting from the center out. You need *at least 40 usable inches (40+″) in width* for the braid run and accent fabrics. Yardages do not allow for fussy cutting, directional prints, or mitering.

Fabric

Buy now

❖ Braid fabrics #1–#12 and center accents: ⅜ yard each

❖ Double accents: 1 yard (3½ yards if you also intend to use it for the outer border; you will have enough fabric for binding as well)

❖ Center squares: ¾ yard

Buy later

❖ Ending triangles: ⅝ yard

❖ Center separators: 1¼ yards

❖ Outline separators and inner border: 1¼ yards (The quilt on page 22 uses 2 different fabrics for the separators and inner border. If you choose to do this, you will need extra fabric.)

❖ Outer border and binding (if not using the same fabric as double accents): 2¾ yards cut lengthwise OR 2½ yards cut crosswise

❖ Backing: 8¼ yards pieced crosswise OR 8¾ yards pieced lengthwise

❖ Batting: 94″ × 101″

Cutting

Braid Fabrics

Number both pieces of each braid fabric as you cut.

Segments

❖ Cut 1 strip 9½″ × width of fabric from each fabric (#1–#12).

Center accents

❖ Cut 1 strip 2½″ × width of fabric from each fabric (#1–#12); cut off about 22″ and discard the smaller piece.

Double Accents, Outer Border, and Binding

Double accents

❖ Cut 12 strips 2½″ × width of fabric.

Outer border

❖ Cut 4 strips 6½″ × length of fabric OR cut 9 strips 6½″ × width of fabric. You will have enough fabric left for binding.

Center Squares

❖ Cut 2 strips 11⅜″; subcut into 4 squares 11⅜″ × 11⅜″.

Ending Triangles

❖ Cut 2 strips 9½″ × width of fabric; subcut into 8 squares 9½″ × 9½″. Cut each square once diagonally to obtain 16 half-square triangles.

Center Separators

❖ Cut 6 strips 3½″ × length of fabric.

Outline Separators and Inner Border

Outline separators

❖ Cut 12 strips 1½″ × length of fabric.

Inner border

❖ Cut 8 strips 1½″ × length of fabric.

Construction

SEGMENTS

1. Sew a strip of double-accent fabric to each 9½″ strip of braid fabric. Do not press.

2. Cut each sewn strip from Step 1 in half at the center fold, making sure that you have *at least 20 usable inches (20+″)* in each half. Make 2 piles of fabric, placing a half-strip of each fabric in each pile.

3. Working with 1 pile only, press the seams toward the braid fabrics. Then cut each piece into 8 segments 2½″. Set aside.

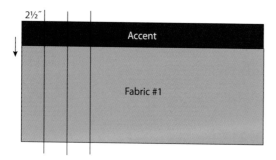

4. In the second pile of braid fabrics, press the seams toward the accent fabrics.

5. Lay out, in order, braid fabrics #1–#12 from Step 4. Then pair the 2½″ center accent strips with them, reversing the order (#12–#1). The 2½″ fabric #12 strip will be paired with the fabric #1 accented strip, the 2½″ fabric #11 strip will be paired with the fabric #2 accented strip, and so on. Pin the pairs together to avoid accidentally rearranging them while you work.

6. Sew a 2½″ center accent strip to the remaining raw edge of each double-accent fabric strip, matching the strips at one end. Press the seams toward the double-accent fabric.

7. Cut each piece into 8 segments 2½″.

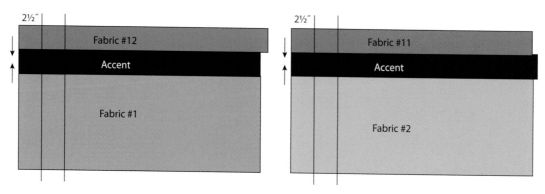

BRAIDS

Read the sections Piecing Center-Out Braids (page 10) and Adding Ending Triangles (page 11).

8. Construct 4 center-out braids, matching the seams as shown.

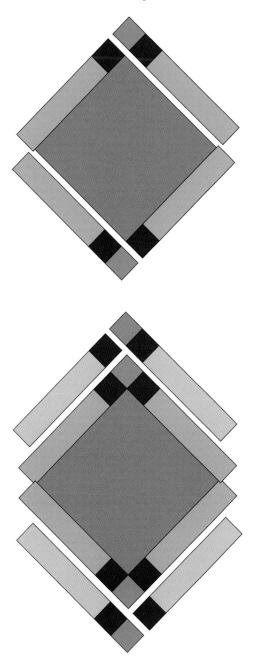

9. Sew the ending triangles to the braids.

Separators, Borders, and Finishing

Read the sections Marking and Trimming (page 12), Separators (page 16), and Borders (page 18).

10. Mark the sides and trim the ends. Measure the length of each braid and write it down.

11. Determine the universal length and write it down.

12. Construct 3 separators and trim them to the universal length.

13. Find and mark the centers of the separators and the braids.

14. Pin a separator to the same side, either left or right, of each of 3 braids, paying attention to the orientation of the center squares if that fabric is directional. Sew.

15. Trim the segment ends where they extend beyond the seams and press the seams toward the separators.

16. Sew the braids into 2 sets of 2 each. Then sew the pairs together.

17. Add borders.

18. Layer with batting and backing, quilt, and bind.

Desert View, 91″ × 99½″ ❖ quilted by Patricia E. Ritter

Variable-Length French Braid

A Bird in the Hand, 78½″ × 89½″ ❖ quilted by Patricia E. Ritter

Fabrics in the braid run are numbered 1 through 6 from the center square out. Although fabric #6 is a longer piece than the others in the braid, you will see less of it because it appears only once in every run; the others each appear twice. Select the braid fabrics first, then the background, accent, and center square fabrics. You need *at least 40 usable inches (40+″) in width* for the braid run, background, and accent fabrics. Yardages do not allow for fussy cutting or directional prints.

Fabric

Buy now

- **Braid fabrics #1, #2, and #6:** ¼ yard each
- **Braid fabrics #3, #4, and #5:** ⅓ yard each
- **Background:** 1⅝ yards (non-directional fabric)
- **Center squares:** ¼ yard (more if you plan to fussy cut)
- **Frames for center squares:** ¼ yard
- **Accents and first border:** 1⅛ yards

Buy later

- **Ending triangles:** ½ yard
- **Center separators:** 1⅛ yards
- **Outline separators, second border, and binding:** 1½ yards
- **Border accents:** scrap at least 2″ × 15″
- **Outer border:** 2¼ yards cut lengthwise OR 1⅝ yards cut crosswise
- **Backing:** 7⅛ yards pieced crosswise in 3 pieces
- **Batting:** 83″ × 94″

Cutting

Braids

Label each braid fabric as you cut.

- Cut 2 strips 3¼″ × width of fabric from fabric #1.
- Cut 2 strips 3¾″ × width of fabric from fabric #2.
- Cut 2 strips 4¼″ × width of fabric from fabric #3.
- Cut 2 strips 4¾″ × width of fabric from fabric #4.
- Cut 2 strips 5¼″ × width of fabric from fabric #5.
- Cut 1 strip 5¾″ × width of fabric from fabric #6.

Background

- Cut 2 strips 5¾″ × width of fabric; place them with the braid fabric #1 strips.
- Cut 2 strips 5¼″ × width of fabric; place them with the braid fabric #2 strips.
- Cut 2 strips 4¾″ × width of fabric; place them with the braid fabric #3 strips.
- Cut 2 strips 4¼″ × width of fabric; place them with the braid fabric #4 strips.
- Cut 2 strips 3¾″ × width of fabric; place them with the braid fabric #5 strips.
- Cut 1 strip 3¼″ × width of fabric; place it with the braid fabric #6 strip.

Center Squares

- Cut 1 strip 6⅜″ × width of fabric; subcut into 4 squares 6⅜″ × 6⅜″.

Frames

- Cut 4 strips 1½″ × width of fabric; subcut 2 strips into 8 pieces 1½″ × 8⅜″ and subcut 2 strips into 8 pieces 1½″ × 6⅜″.

Accents and First Border

Accents

❖ Cut 6 strips 2½″ × width of fabric; cut 1 strip in half on the center fold, making sure that 1 of the pieces is at least 20″. Discard the other piece.

First border

❖ From the remaining accent fabric, cut 9 strips 2″ × width of fabric.

Ending Triangles

❖ Cut 2 strips 7″ × width of fabric; subcut into 8 squares 7″ × 7″. Cut each square once diagonally to obtain 16 half-square triangles.

Center Separators

❖ Cut 6 strips 4½″ × length of fabric.

Outline Separators, Second Border, and Binding

❖ Cut 15 strips 1¼″ × length of fabric for the outline separators and second border. You will have enough fabric left for binding.

Border Accents

❖ From a scrap 2″ × 15″, subcut 4 squares 2″ × 2″ and 4 squares 1¼″ × 1¼″.

Outer Border

❖ From 2¼ yards cut 4 strips 6½″ × length of fabric OR from 1⅝ yards cut 8 strips 6½″ × width of fabric.

Construction

CENTER SQUARES AND SEGMENTS

> **note**
>
> The background is referred to as BG throughout the instructions. Arrows indicate pressing directions.

1. Sew a frame strip 1½″ × 6⅜″ to any side of each center square. Sew another strip to each opposite side. Press the seams toward the frames.

2. Sew a 1½″ × 8⅜″ strip to a raw edge of each 6⅜″ × 6⅜″ center square. Sew a remaining 1½″ × 8⅜″ strip to the last raw edge of each square. Press the seams toward the frames and set aside.

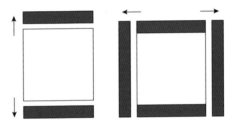

3. Sew each BG strip to its respective braid fabric strip (5¾″ BG strip to braid fabric #1, 5¼″ BG strip to braid fabric #2, etc.), matching the long edges and an end. Do not press.

4. Separate fabrics #1–#5 into 2 piles, with 1 strip of each fabric in each pile. Finger-press the fabric #6 + BG strip in half, making sure there is at least 20″ of usable width of the entire unit on each side of the fold. Cut the strip in half on the fold and place a half with each pile.

5. Press the seams in one pile toward the braid fabrics.

6. Cut each strip set of fabrics #1–#5 in the pressed pile into 16 segments 2½″ to obtain 16 segments of each fabric. Cut the fabric #6 strip set into 8 segments 2½″.

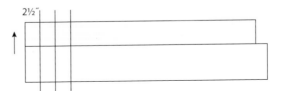

7. Sew the half-strip of accent fabric to the fabric #6 edge of the unpressed half-strip set of fabric #6 + BG. Press both seams toward the BG and set aside.

8. Sew an accent strip to the braid fabric edge of each unpressed strip set of fabrics #1–#5, matching the long edges and an end. Press all the seams toward the BG strips and place them with the accented half-strip set of fabric #6.

9. Cut each strip set of fabrics #1–#5 into 16 segments 2½″ to obtain 16 accented segments of each fabric. Cut the fabric #6 strip set into 8 accented segments 2½″.

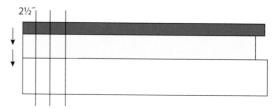

BRAIDS

Read the sections Piecing Center-Out Braids (page 10) and Adding Ending Triangles (page 11).

10. Construct 4 center-out braids using the following sequence: 1-2-3-4-5-6-5-4-3-2-1.

11. Add ending triangles to both ends of each braid.

MARKING, TRIMMING, AND SEPARATORS

Read the sections Marking and Trimming (page 12) and Separators (page 16).

12. Mark the sides, trim the ends, measure the lengths, and determine the universal length. Save the universal length number to use when you construct the borders.

13. Construct 3 separator bands and trim them to the universal length.

14. Find and mark the centers of the separators and the braids.

15. Pin a separator to the same side, either left or right, of each of 3 braids, paying attention to the orientation of the center squares if that fabric is directional. Sew.

16. Trim the segment ends where they extend beyond the seams, and press the seams toward the separators.

17. Sew the braids into 2 pairs; then sew the pairs together.

Borders and Finishing

18. Measure the width of the quilt from pencil line to pencil line across the center without stretching it. Write down the number.

19. Sew 2″ first border (blue) strips end to end to obtain enough length and cut as follows:

a. 2 pieces 2″ × universal length, labeled #7

b. 2 pieces 2″ × width of quilt, labeled #8

c. 8 pieces 2″ × 6½″, labeled #9

20. If cutting the outer border from 4 strips 6½″ × length of fabric, cut as follows:

a. 2 strips 6½″ × universal length, labeled #14

b. 2 squares 6½″ × 6½″ from each of the 2 remaining strips, labeled #13

c. 2 strips 6½″ × width of quilt, labeled #10 (using the remainder of the strips from Step b)

If you are cutting from 8 strips 6½″ × width of fabric, first sew them end to end to obtain enough length. Then cut #10, #13, and #14 pieces as above.

21. Sew 1¼″ second border (brown) strips end to end to obtain enough length and cut as follows:

a. 2 pieces 1¼″ × universal length plus 3″ (twice the finished width of the first border), labeled #11

b. 2 pieces 1¼″ × width of quilt plus 3″, labeled E2

c. 8 pieces 1¼″ × 6½″, labeled #12

22. Sew border #7 pieces to the sides of the quilt as if they were separators (see Separators, page 16). Trim the segment ends and press the seams toward the borders.

23. Construct the end borders as follows:

a. Sew a 2″ × 2″ border accent square to each end of each #8 unit. Press the seams toward the #8 pieces and label the entire unit E1 (end, first border).

b. Sew a #9 piece to each end of each #10 piece. Press the seams toward the #10 pieces and label the entire unit E3.

c. Sew an E1 unit to each E2 piece, matching the ends, centers, and long edges. Press the seams toward the E2 pieces.

d. Sew an E3 unit to the E2 edge of each E1/E2 unit, matching the ends, centers, and long edges and aligning the seams near the ends of the E1 and E3 units. Press the seams toward the E3 units. These are the end borders.

24. Sew an end border completed in Step 23 to each end of the braid top, matching the ends, centers, and seams. Press the seams toward the borders.

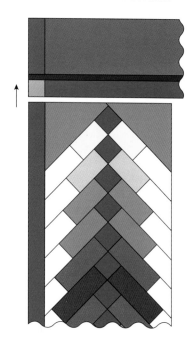

25. Construct the side borders as follows:

a. Sew a 1¼″ × 1¼″ border accent square to each end of each #11 piece. Sew a #12 piece to the opposite edge of each accent square. Press both seams toward the #11 pieces and label the entire unit S2 (side, second border).

b. Sew a remaining #12 piece to an edge of each #13 piece, paying attention to the orientation if the outer border fabric is directional.

c. Sew a remaining #9 piece to each end of each #14 piece.

d. Sew the #12 edge of the #12/#13 unit to the #9 edge of the #9/#14 unit. Press all the seams toward the #13 pieces and label the entire unit S3.

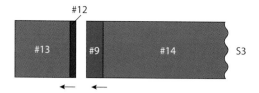

e. Sew each S2 unit to an S3 unit, matching the ends, centers, and seams. Press the seams toward S3.

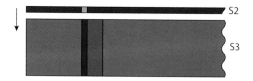

26. Sew the side borders to the sides of the top, matching the ends, centers, and seams and aligning the seams near the end of the S1 and S3 units. Press the seams toward the outer edges of the top.

27. Layer with batting and backing, quilt, and bind.

It's a Gray Area, 95½″ × 103″ ❖ quilted by Marybeth O'Halloran

Leapin' Lizards, 44″ × 60½″ ❖ quilted by Patricia E. Ritter

Scrappy French Braid

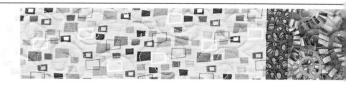

It's Easy Being Green ❖ 36¾″ × 46½″

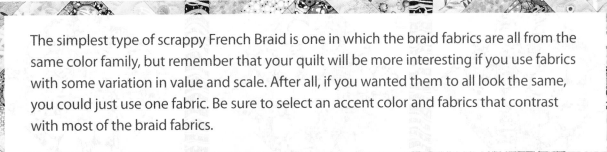

The simplest type of scrappy French Braid is one in which the braid fabrics are all from the same color family, but remember that your quilt will be more interesting if you use fabrics with some variation in value and scale. After all, if you wanted them to all look the same, you could just use one fabric. Be sure to select an accent color and fabrics that contrast with most of the braid fabrics.

Fabric

Buy now

- **Braid fabrics:** 16 fat eighths or 16 large scraps at least 6½″ × at least 12″*

- **Accents:** 8 scraps 1¾″ × at least 12″ OR ¼ yard, straight or fat, of a single fabric

- **Center squares:** ¼ yard, straight or fat

  Slightly smaller scraps will work well for this quilt as long as one dimension is at least 6½″. Adjust the sewing technique for the segments and make sure you have 48 segments with accents and 48 without accents before beginning to piece the braid.

Buy later

- **Ending triangles:** ¼ yard

- **Separators and binding:** ½ yard

- **Inner border:** ¼ yard

- **Outer border:** 1¼ yards cut lengthwise OR ⅝ yard cut crosswise

- **Border corners:** 1 fat eighth

- **Backing:** 1½ yards

- **Batting:** 41″ × 51″

Cutting

Braids

- Cut 1 strip 6½″ × width of fabric from each fat eighth. If you are using scraps, cut 16 pieces 6½″ × at least 12″.

Accents

- **From scraps:** Cut 1 piece 1¾″ × at least 12″ from each.

OR

- **From a straight quarter:** Cut 3 strips 1¾″ × width of fabric; subcut each strip into 3 equal pieces, each about 1¾″ × 13+″.

OR

- **From a fat quarter:** Cut 8 strips 1¾″ × width of fabric.

Center Squares

- Cut 1 strip 6⅜″ × width of fabric; subcut into 3 squares 6⅜″ × 6⅜″.

Ending Triangles

- Cut 1 strip 6″ × width of fabric; subcut into 6 squares 6″ × 6″. Cut each triangle once diagonally to obtain 12 half-square triangles.

Separators and Binding

- Cut 2 strips 1½″ × width of fabric. You will have enough fabric left for binding.

Inner Border

- Cut 5 strips 1½″ × width of fabric.

Outer Borders

- From 1¼ yards cut 4 strips 4½″ × length of fabric OR from ⅝ yard cut 4 strips 4½″ × width of fabric.

Border Corners

- Cut 1 strip 4½″ × width of fabric; subcut into 4 squares 4½″ × 4½″.

Construction

SEGMENTS

1. Sort the braid fabrics into 2 piles of 8 strips each, distributing the more obtrusive fabrics equally.

2. From each fabric in *1 pile only*, subcut 6 segments 1¾". Set aside.

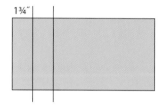

3. Sew an accent strip to each strip of fabric in the remaining pile, matching the long edges. Press the seams toward the braid fabrics.

4. From each accented braid fabric, subcut 6 segments 1¾". Set aside.

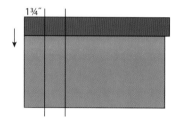

BRAIDS

Read the sections Piecing Center-Out Braids (page 10) and Adding Ending Triangles (page 11).

> **note**
>
> To distribute the fabrics more evenly among the braids, divide the segments into 3 groups, placing 2 segments of each unaccented braid fabric and 2 segments of each accented braid fabric in each group. Use 1 group for each braid.

5. Construct 3 center-out braids. The braid segments are not added in any particular order, but try to distribute the various fabrics as evenly as possible.

6. Sew the ending triangles to the braids.

MARKING, TRIMMING, AND SEPARATORS

Read the sections Marking and Trimming (page 12) and Separators (page 16).

7. Mark the sides and trim the ends. Measure the length of each braid and write it down.

8. Determine the universal length and write it down.

9. Cut 2 separator strips to the universal length.

10. Find and mark the centers of the separators and the braids.

11. Sew a separator to the same side, right or left, of each of 2 braids, paying attention to the orientation of the center squares if that fabric is directional.

12. Trim the segment ends where they extend beyond the seams and press the seams toward the separators.

13. Sew 2 of the braids into a pair. Then add the third, pressing and trimming as in Step 12.

14. Measure the width of the top across the center, from pencil line to pencil line, and write it down.

BORDERS AND FINISHING

Read the section Borders (page 18).

15. Sew an inner border strip to each of 2 outer border strips. Press the seams toward the outer borders. Cut the borders to the universal length.

16. Sew a border to each side of the quilt top, matching, pinning, sewing, and trimming as for the separators.

17. From 1 strip of inner border fabric, cut 4 pieces 1½″ × 4½″. Sew 1 piece to an edge of each border corner square. If your fabric is directional, sew the inner border piece to the inner *side* edge of each square with both prints facing the same direction. Press the seams toward the squares.

18. Cut the remaining 2 outer border strips to the width of the quilt you wrote down in Step 14.

19. Sew the inner border edge of a corner square piece from Step 17 to each end of each outer border strip. Press the seams toward the inner border.

20. Measure the length of the border. Cut the remaining 2 inner border strips to the same length. Sew an inner border strip to each pieced outer border, matching the ends and centers and paying attention to the orientation if your fabric is directional. Press the seams toward the inner borders.

21. Sew the top and bottom borders to the quilt, matching the centers, ends, and inner border seamlines. Press the seams toward the border.

Quilt top

22. Layer with batting and backing, quilt, and bind.

Fruit of the Vine, 74″ × 75″

Made for a friend who loves wine, purple, and square quilts.

Black and Gray and Red All Over, 93″ × 95″

The Big Apple, 62½″ × 76″ ❖ quilted by Heather Spence

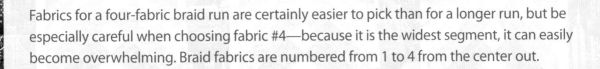

Fabrics for a four-fabric braid run are certainly easier to pick than for a longer run, but be especially careful when choosing fabric #4—because it is the widest segment, it can easily become overwhelming. Braid fabrics are numbered from 1 to 4 from the center out.

Fabric

- ❖ Braid fabrics #1 and #4: ⅝ yard each
- ❖ Braid fabrics #2 and #3: ⅞ yard each
- ❖ Accents and inner border: ¾ yard
- ❖ Outer borders, center separators, ending triangles, and center squares: 2⅝ yards

> ## note
>
> If you want to use different fabrics for each of these components, you will need:
>
> - ❖ **Center squares:** ⅓ yard
> - ❖ **Ending triangles:** ⅝ yard
> - ❖ **Separators and outer borders:** 2¼ yards

- ❖ Outline separators and binding: 1 yard
- ❖ Backing: 4½ yards pieced lengthwise
- ❖ Batting: 67″ × 80″

Cutting

Braids

Braid fabrics #1 and #4

- ❖ From each fabric, cut 2 strips 9″ × width of fabric.

Braid fabrics #2 and #3

- ❖ From each fabric, cut 3 strips 9″ × width of fabric.

Accents and Inner Border

Accents

- ❖ Cut 1 strip 2¾″ × width of fabric; place it with braid fabric #4.
- ❖ Cut 2 strips 2¼″ × width of fabric; place them with braid fabric #3.
- ❖ Cut 2 strips 1¾″ × width of fabric; place them with braid fabric #2.
- ❖ Cut 1 strip 1¼″ × width of fabric; place it with braid fabric #1.

Inner Border

- ❖ Cut 6 strips 1½″ × width of fabric.

Outer Borders, Center Separators, Ending Triangles, and Center Squares

Cut in the order listed and label each component as you cut. These instructions are for fabric with a directional print.

Outer borders

- ❖ Cut 3 strips 5½″ × width of fabric for the end borders.
- ❖ Cut 2 strips 5½″ × length of fabric for the side borders.

Center separators

- ❖ Cut 2 strips 4½″ × length of fabric.

Ending triangles

- ❖ Cut 3 strips 8″ × width of fabric; subcut into 6 squares 8″ × 8″. Cut 3 squares diagonally in one direction and 3 in the opposite direction to maintain the correct orientation.

Center squares

- ❖ Cut 3 squares 8½″ × 8½″ *on point* (sides on the bias) from the remaining fabric, fussy cutting if desired.

Outline Separators and Binding

- ❖ Cut 8 strips 1½″ × length of fabric. You will have enough fabric left for binding.

Construction

SEGMENTS

Press the seams in Steps 1–8 toward the braid fabrics.

1. Sew the 2¾″ accent strip to a braid fabric #4 strip; press. Subcut it into 12 segments 2¾″. Subcut the unaccented strip into 12 segments 2¾″.

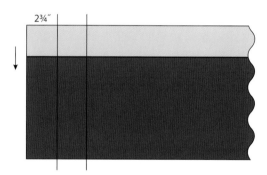

2. Cut a 2¼″ accent strip in half; cut a fabric #3 strip in half. Sew a half-strip of accent fabric to a half-strip of the braid fabric; press. Sew a full 2¼″ accent strip to a full strip of braid fabric; press. Subcut the accented strips into 24 segments 2¼″. Subcut the unaccented strips into 24 segments 2¼″.

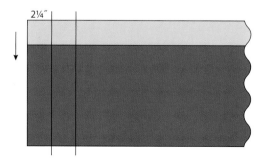

3. Cut a 1¾″ accent strip in half; cut a fabric #2 strip in half. Sew a half-strip of accent fabric to a half-strip of the braid fabric; press. Sew the full 1¾″ accent strip to a full strip of braid fabric; press. Subcut the accented strips into 24 segments 1¾″. Subcut the unaccented strips into 24 segments 1¾″.

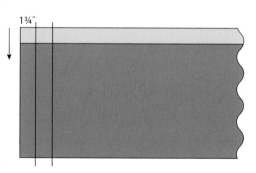

4. Sew the 1¼″ accent strip to a braid fabric #1 strip; press. Subcut it into 18 segments 1¼″. Subcut the unaccented strip into 18 segments 1¼″.

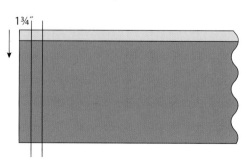

BRAIDS

Read the sections Piecing Center-Out Braids (page 10) and Adding Ending Triangles (page 11).

5. Construct 3 center-out braids, adding the segments in numerical order and reverse numerical order, twice, as follows: 1-2-3-4-3-2-1-2-3-4-3-2-1. The first segments are about ½″ longer than the center squares. This braid is designed to allow the center square to float a bit, and the first set of segments will overlap at the ends as shown in the illustration below.

6. Add ending triangles to both ends of each braid.

MARKING, TRIMMING, SEPARATORS, BORDERS, AND FINISHING

Read the sections Marking and Trimming (page 12), Separators (page 16), and Borders (page 18).

7. Mark the sides, *with a change*: Ignore the instruction about placing the ¼″ line of the ruler at the outer point of the center square, as directed. Instead, just draw the line straight down each side, using the accent squares as your guide. *NOTE:* The segments don't all extend to the same line on the mat; align the longest ones.

Depending on your seam allowance, there should be about ½″ to ¾″ of braid fabric on each side of the braid between the corner of the center square and the pencil line.

8. Trim the ends. Measure the length of each braid and write it down.

9. Determine the universal length and write it down.

10. Construct 2 separators and trim them to the universal length.

11. Find and mark the centers of the separators and the braids.

12. Sew a separator to the same side, left or right, of each of 2 braids, paying attention to the orientation of the center squares if that fabric is directional.

13. Trim the segment ends where they extend beyond the seams and press the seams toward the separators.

14. Sew 2 of the braids into a pair. Then add the third, pressing and trimming as in Steps 11–13.

15. Sew the 3 end border strips together end to end. Cut as needed.

16. Add the borders.

17. Layer with batting and backing, quilt, and bind.

Still Spring, 95½″ × 95½″ ❖ quilted by Patricia E. Ritter

French Braid Stars

French Braid Stars: Spring, 57˝ × 74½˝

This quilt consists of four short center-out braids with star blocks as center squares, and four short basic braids with half-star blocks as starting triangles. The center squares and the starting triangles could be replaced with a single piece of fabric, 10″ blocks, or 8″ blocks with 1″ frames (*French Braid Sampler*, page 54). To get the effect in the photo, buy ombré fabric that is *all one color*. You need *at least 40 usable inches (40+″) in width* for the two ombré fabrics.

Fabric

- Blue star backgrounds, braid segments, accents, outer borders, and setting triangles: 3⅛ yards blue ombré

- Green star backgrounds, braid segments, accents, setting triangles, and inner border cornerstones: 2⅜ yards green ombré

- Star centers: ¼ yard nondirectional print

- Separators, inner border, star points, and binding: 2 yards*

- Backing: 4½ yards pieced lengthwise OR 3½ yards pieced crosswise

- Batting: 61″ × 79″

* In the photo, this fabric is a dark gray ombré, but it is not necessary to use an ombré fabric.

Cutting

note

Cutting instructions for the ombré fabrics are written as if the color progression runs from dark on both edges to light in the center. If the color progression on your fabric is reversed, change the cutting instructions accordingly. The illustrations show the fabric after it has been folded at the center, and instructions are written as if you are cutting two layers at once.

Star Backgrounds, Braid Segments, Accents, Outer Borders, and Setting Triangles (Blue Ombré)

From the 112″ length, cut off a piece 40″ × width of fabric. Fold it in half lengthwise at the lightest (or darkest) part of the color, which is sometimes slightly off-center. *Measure to make sure you have at least 20″ of usable width on each side of the fold.* If you don't have 20+″ on one side, refold the fabric so that you do—it's more important to have enough width than to have the exact coloration. Cut off the fold, removing as little as possible—about 2 threads' width.

Star backgrounds

Note: You are cutting through 2 matching layers of fabric for all of the following cuts.

- From the lightest part of the fabric, center or selvages, make a cut 3½″ × length of fabric to yield 2 strips, first making sure that you will still have more than 16″ in width left on each side after you cut. From each 3½″ strip, cut 4 rectangles 3½″ × 5″ and 4 squares 3½″ × 3½″, for a total of 8 rectangles and 8 squares.

Braid segments and accents

❖ From leftover fabric, make
2 cuts 10⅝″ × the remaining
width of fabric (16+″) to obtain
4 strips for braid segments and
make 2 cuts 2″ × the remaining
width of fabric to obtain 4
strips for accents.

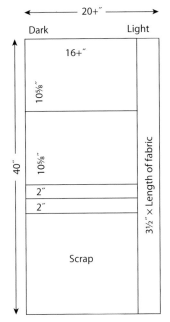

Cutting 2 layers of matching fabric

Outer border

❖ From the second, larger piece
of fabric, approximately
72″ × width of fabric, first fold
at the center and trim from
the fold as you did for the blue
ombré (page 46). Then make
2 cuts 5½″ × length of fabric
from the darkest part of the
fabric to yield 4 strips for outer
borders.

Setting triangles

❖ Measuring from the remaining
darker edge, make a cut
8¼″ × length of fabric. Use
the darker edge of the layered
strips as a baseline, along with
either a large 45-45-90 triangle
ruler or the 45° and 90° lines
on your standard ruler, to cut
4 pairs of quarter-square triangles, each with a 16½″ base.

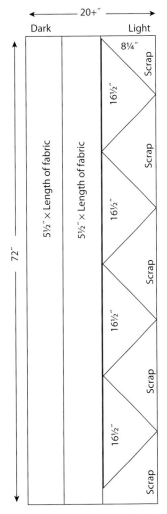

Cut 2 layers of matching fabric.

Star Backgrounds, Braid Segments, Accents, Setting Triangles, and Inner Border Cornerstones (Green Ombré)

First fold at the center (the lightest or
darkest part) and trim off the fold as
you did for the blue fabric (page 46).

Star backgrounds

❖ From the lightest part of the
fabric, make a cut 3½″ × length
of fabric to yield 2 strips, first
making sure that you will
still have more than 16″ in
width left on each side after
you cut. From *each* 3½″ strip,
cut 8 rectangles 3½″ × 5″ and
10 squares 3½″ × 3½″, for
a total of 16 rectangles and
20 squares.

Braid segments and accents

❖ From the rest of the fabric, make
4 cuts 10⅝″ × the remaining
width of fabric to obtain 8
strips for braid segments. Then
make 1 cut 2″ × the remaining
width of fabric to obtain
2 strips for accents.

Setting and ending triangles

❖ Measuring from the remaining
lighter edge, make 1 cut
8½″ × length of fabric to yield
2 strips; subcut 2 pairs of half-
square triangles 8½″, orienting
them as shown, for ending
triangles. Cut the remainder of
the 8½″ strips down to 8¼″. Use
the lighter edges of these strips
as a baseline, along with either
a large 45-45-90 triangle ruler
or the 45° and 90° lines on your
standard ruler, to cut 1 pair

of quarter-square triangles, each with a 16½″ base, for side setting triangles.

You will cut the 4 small squares for the inner border cornerstones in Step 28 (page 54).

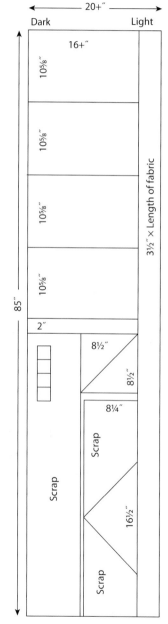

Cut 2 layers of matching fabric.

Star Centers

❖ Cut 1 strip 8″ × width of fabric; subcut into 1 square 8″ × 8″ and 4 squares 5″ × 5″. Cut the 8″ square diagonally twice to yield 4 quarter-square triangles.

Separators, Inner Border, Star Points, and Binding

Separators and inner border

❖ Cut off a strip 15″ × length of fabric and set it aside until Step 28 (page 54).

Star points

❖ From the rest of the fabric, cut 6 strips 2¾″ × remaining width of fabric; subcut into 48 squares 2¾″ × 2¾″. You will have enough fabric left for binding.

Construction

STARS

The star points are intended to float on the background. This method of construction is quicker than most but less accurate than some. For this reason, they're made slightly larger than necessary and then cut down to exactly the required size.

Sewing diagonally across the square will be easier if you place a piece of masking tape about 4″ long on the bed of your sewing machine. Align one edge of the tape with the machine needle just in front of the feed. Use the edge of the tape as a sewing guide to sew across the corners of the squares. An alternate method is to draw a line from one corner to the opposite corner of each star point square.

1. Match the corner of 1 star point square 2¾″ × 2¾″ with a star background rectangle 3½″ × 5″ as shown. Align the beginning point of the star square with the machine needle; align the opposite point with the edge of the tape. Sew diagonally across the center of the point square from raw edge to raw edge, keeping the destination corner at the edge of the tape. Sew all the rectangles of both colors this way.

2. Fold the top center corner of the square down over the outer corner along the seamline to form a triangle. Align the outer edges of the triangles. Press. Some quilters like to leave both layers under the pressed point, and you may want to do this to use them as a reference line if your pressed point doesn't quite reach the others. But to reduce both weight and bulk, you may also flip up the point and trim off the extra star point corner (the middle layer). If you are confident that the pressed point is exactly aligned with the rectangle corner, trim off both the extra star corner and the rectangle corner. If you decide to trim, place the ¼″ line of your ruler on the stitching and trim off the corner. Then fold the point back down.

3. Repeat the process with the rest of the star point squares, aligning them with the adjacent long side of the background rectangle. Press as in Step 2 and trim if desired.

4. Select 4 blue point units and 8 green point units. Sew a background square to each end of each rectangle to make the star sides as shown. Press the seams toward the squares.

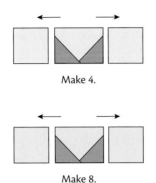

Make 4.

Make 8.

5. Select 2 star centers and 4 blue point units. Sew a blue point unit to each of 2 opposite sides of each star center. Repeat using the remaining 2 star centers and 4 of the 8 green point units. Press the seams toward the star centers.

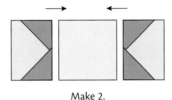

Make 2.

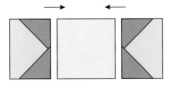

Make 2.

6. Sew 2 star sides to each unit from Step 5, matching the colors, seams, and outer edges. Press the seams toward the centers. You will have 2 stars with blue backgrounds and 2 with green backgrounds.

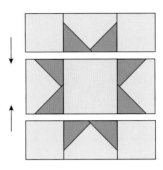

Make 2.

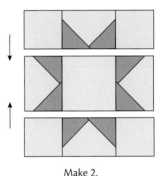

Make 2.

7. Trim the star blocks down to 10½″ × 10½″. You will be cutting off about ¼″ on each of the 4 sides, and the cuts should be 3″ or very close to 3″ from the seams between the star center and the star sides for all 4 cuts.

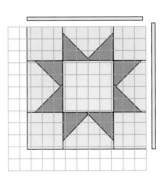

8. Sew each of the last 4 green background squares to the left edge of a remaining green point unit as shown. Press the seams toward the squares.

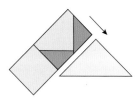

Make 4.

9. Sew each of these units to the left shorter side of a star center triangle, matching the top ends as shown. Press the seams toward the triangles.

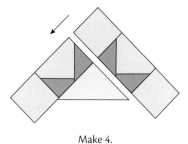

10. Sew a remaining green star side from Step 4 to the right shorter side of each star center triangle, matching the top ends and seams as shown. Press the seams toward the triangles.

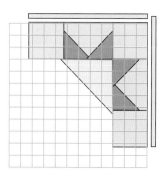

Make 4.

11. Turn the unit and use a square ruler to trim the 2 star point edges as in Step 7. Use the 3″ line on the square ruler as before.

SEGMENTS

12. Select 4 of the green 10⅝″ strips. Sew the long edge of a blue 2″ strip to each green strip, matching the light end of the blue strip to the dark end of the green strip and orienting both pieces exactly as shown in the illustration after Step 13, with the lighter end of the larger piece on the left and the lighter end of the smaller piece on the right. Your quilt will not look like the photo if you rotate either piece. Press the seams toward the larger pieces.

13. Cut each of the strips into 8 segments 2″, stacking if desired. *Before you move anything,* number the pieces from lightest green to darkest as follows: 1, 5, 2, 6, 3, 7, 4, 8. Then cut the 4 green unaccented 10⅝″ strips, orienting them in the same direction as the accented strips and labeling them as you go. As you cut more segments, be sure to put them into the appropriate stacks. You should have 4 segments with accents and 4 segments without accents in each of 8 stacks.

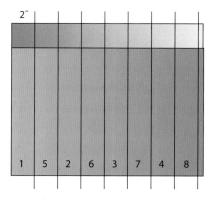

14. Select 2 of the blue 10⅝″ strips. Sew the long edge of a green 2″ strip to each blue strip, matching the light end of the green strip to the dark end of the blue strip, *orienting them as shown in the diagram above*: larger light on left, smaller light on right. Press the seams toward the larger piece.

15. Cut and label the pieces exactly as in Step 13. This time you will have 2 segments with and 2 without accents in each stack.

BRAIDS

Read the sections Piecing Center-Out Braids (page 10) and Adding Ending Triangles (page 11).

Because it is easy to rotate a segment, you may find it helpful to lay out the braids on a table or design wall before sewing them.

16. Use the 2 blue background stars as the center squares for 2 center-out braids, each with a 4-fabric blue braid run. Make one end of each braid using fabrics 1, 2, 3, and 4, and the other end using fabrics 5, 6, 7, and 8. This is less confusing if you sew the 1–4 segments to both stars before starting on the 5–8 segments. The 2 ends will look very similar. The unaccented segments have a lighter edge and a darker edge; place the lighter edges nearer the center star as you add them. It is sometimes easier to tell which edge is which by looking at the back of the fabric.

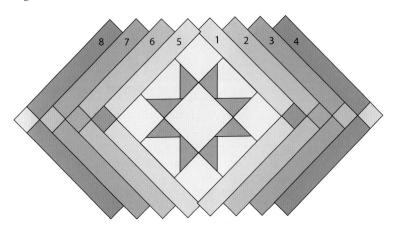

17. Sew 2 green ending triangles to the 1-2-3-4 segment end of each blue braid.

18. Sew a green setting triangle to the top left side at the other end of each blue braid, matching the 90° angles. Press the seams toward the triangles.

19. Sew the 2 braid halves together on the diagonal seam, matching the existing triangle seams. Press the seam in either direction.

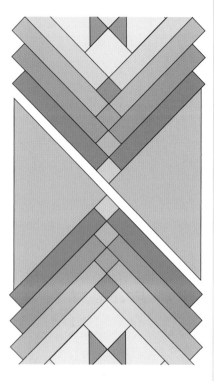

20. Repeat Step 16 using the 2 stars with the green background and the green braid segments 5, 6, 7, and 8 on *both* ends of the braid.

21. Read the section Piecing Basic Braids (page 8). Then use the green background half-stars as the starting triangles for 4 basic braids, each with a 4-fabric green braid run using segments 1, 2, 3, and 4.

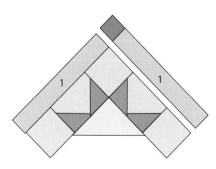

22. Sew a blue setting triangle to the top left side of each green center-out (full star) braid as shown. Turn the 2 braids 180° and sew a blue setting triangle to each top left side on the opposite ends. Press the seams toward the triangles.

23. Sew a blue setting triangle to the top left edge of each green basic (half-star) braid as shown. Press the seams toward the triangles.

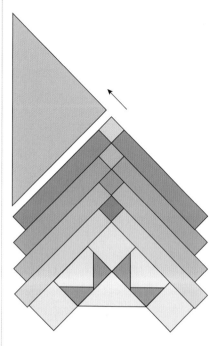

24. Sew a half-star basic braid to each end of each green full-star center-out braid, matching and pressing the seams as in Step 19.

MARKING AND TRIMMING

Read the section Marking and Trimming (page 12).

25. Mark the sides, trim the ends, and measure the braid columns. Trim the ends of the half-star columns as for basic braids, first making sure that your cut will be ¼″ past the bottom edge of the star point seams. Determine the universal length.

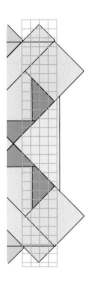

26. Fold the long outer edge of each interior setting triangle (the 2 green and 4 blue that will be near the center of the finished quilt) to find its center; make a mark there on the line you have already drawn.

SEPARATORS AND FINISHING

Read the sections Separators (page 16) and Borders (page 18).

> **note**
>
> The separator width must be adjusted to align the setting triangle seams in the adjacent columns. By following the instructions in Steps 27 and 28 you will determine the separator width required to align the seams exactly. Read the steps and decide whether this process seems too cumbersome. If so, just cut 6 strips 1¾″ × length of fabric from the 15″ strip of star point / separator fabric, and 4 squares 1¾″ × 1¾″ from the darker portion of the leftover green ombré fabric and proceed to Step 29.

27. Lay out 2 braids side by side on a table. You need to see at least half the length of the braid. Adjust the space between the braids until the diagonal setting triangle seams align for as much of the column as you can see. Be sure that the marked lines on the outer edges of the 2 columns are straight and parallel to each other.

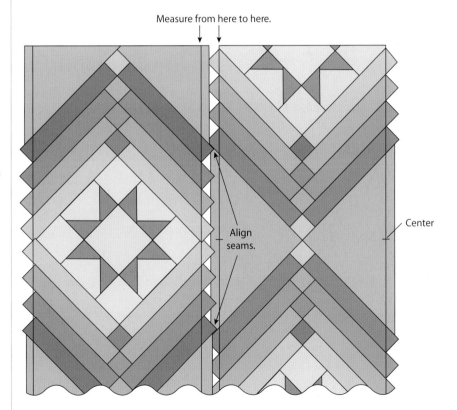

Measure from here to here.

Align seams.

Center

28. Measure the distance between the lines at several places down the braid length. Add 1″ (not ½″) to determine the separator width. Round it off to the nearest ¼″ (usually 1½″ to 2″) and cut 4 squares this size from a darker portion of the leftover green ombré fabric. From the 15″ strip you cut from the star point / separator fabric, cut 6 strips the separator width × length of fabric. Two strips will be separators and 4 will be inner borders.

29. Cut down 4 of the separator/border strips to the universal length determined in Step 25 (page 53).

30. Sew a green square to each end of 2 of these strips and set aside to use as the side inner borders.

31. Pin and sew separators to 1 blue column and 1 green column. Trim the segment ends.

32. Sew the columns together, placing the center mark at the edge of the setting triangle directly across the separator from the outer corner of a star block in the adjacent column. Pin, sew, and trim as above.

33. Measure the width of the quilt through the center and trim the 2 remaining inner border strips to this length. Sew to the top and bottom of the quilt.

34. Add the remaining borders, being sure to match the cornerstone / top (or bottom) border seams and the braid / side border seams.

35. Layer with batting and backing, quilt, and bind.

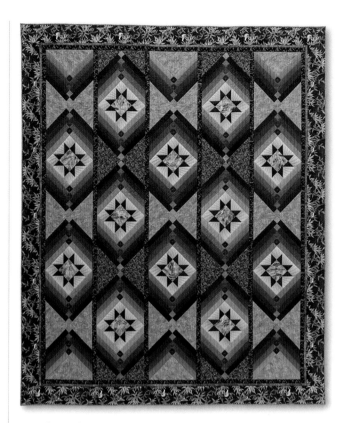

French Braid Stars: Winter, 89½″ × 108″ ❖ quilted by Marybeth O'Halloran

French Braid Sampler, 56″ × 73½″

Crazy Braid

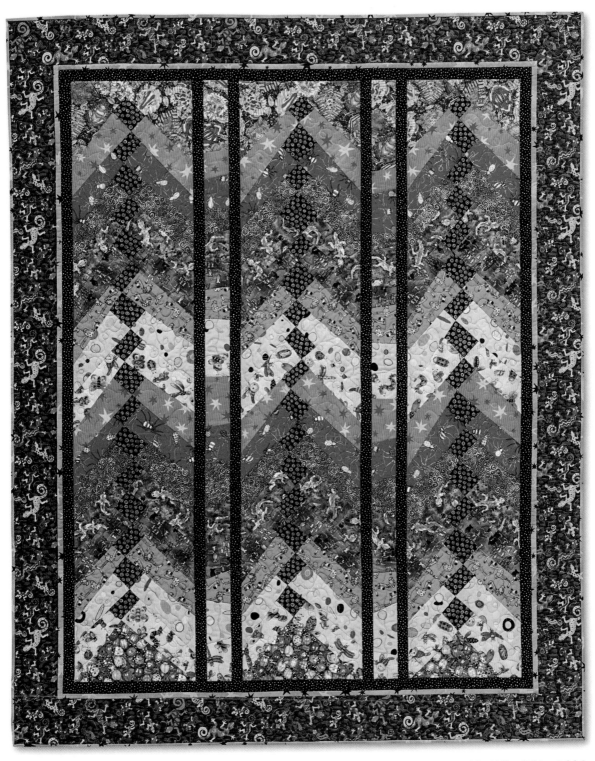

Crazy Braid, 51½″ × 63″ (variable)

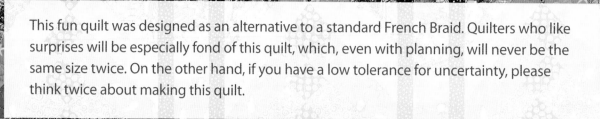

This fun quilt was designed as an alternative to a standard French Braid. Quilters who like surprises will be especially fond of this quilt, which, even with planning, will never be the same size twice. On the other hand, if you have a low tolerance for uncertainty, please think twice about making this quilt.

Fabric

Buy now

- ❖ **Braid and pieced separators:** ½ yard each of 8 fabrics
- ❖ **Accents:** ½ yard
- ❖ **Starting triangles:** ¼ yard

Buy later

- ❖ **Ending triangles and separator tops:** ⅜ yard
- ❖ **Outline separators and inner border:** ⅝ yard
- ❖ **Second border and binding:** ¾ yard
- ❖ **Outer border:** 1¾ yards cut lengthwise OR 1 yard cut crosswise*
- ❖ **Backing:** 3¼ yards pieced crosswise OR 4 yards pieced lengthwise*
- ❖ **Batting:** 56″ × 67″*

Because the finished size of the quilt varies, it is especially important to wait until you're further along to purchase these components, and then only after rechecking the requirements for your own quilt's size.

Cutting

Braids

Label the fabrics #1–#8.

Segments

- ❖ From each fabric, cut 1 strip 10″ × width of fabric; cut each strip in half on the center fold to yield 2 strips 10″ × 20+″.

Pieced separators

- ❖ From the remaining piece of each fabric, cut 1 strip 2″–5″ × half the fabric width. The cuts to make the strip should not be parallel; the narrower end should be no less than 2″ wide and the wider end no wider than 5″. Do not cut every fabric exactly the same.

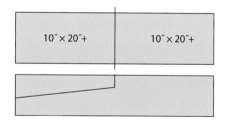

Accents

- ❖ Cut 4 strips 4″ × width of fabric. Cut each strip in half at the center fold to obtain 8 strips 4″ × 20+″.

Starting Triangles

- ❖ Trim off the raw edges of the ¼ yard. Open it and use a ruler to make a diagonal cut. Using the lines on the ruler or the 90° angle on a triangle ruler, cut a 90° angle for the top of the starting triangle. The angles of the 2 other corners don't have to be equal, nor do the sides of the triangles. Cut 2 more triangles for a total of 3; they will not all be the same size or shape, but one angle of each triangle should be 90°.

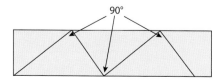

Ending Triangles and Separator Tops

Ending triangles

❖ Cut 1 strip 11″ × width of fabric; subcut into 3 squares 11″ × 11″. Cut each square once diagonally to yield 6 half-square triangles.

Separator tops

❖ Cut 2 pieces 2¾″ × 11″ from the remainder of the strip.

Outline Separators and Inner Border**

❖ Cut 11 strips 1½″ × width of fabric.

Second Border and Binding**

❖ Cut 6 strips 1″ × width of fabric. (You will have enough fabric left for the binding.)

Outer Border**

❖ Cut 4 strips 4¾″ × length of fabric OR 6 strips 4¾″ × width of fabric.

** *The number of strips is based on the size of the quilt in the photo. Although your quilt top should be close to the same size, please measure it and refigure before cutting.*

Construction

SEGMENTS

1. Separate the braid segment fabrics into 2 piles, with 1 piece of each fabric in each pile.

2. Sew an accent strip to each braid fabric in 1 of the piles, matching the long edges. Press the seams toward the braid fabrics.

3. Cut the unaccented braid fabrics at non-90° angles, alternating the wider and narrower ends as shown and varying the cut distances from 2″ to 3½″. Cut 6 segments from each fabric.

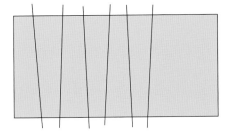

4. Cut the accented braid fabrics as above, again cutting 6 segments from each fabric.

BRAIDS

Read the section Piecing Basic Braids (page 8).

The general idea is the same as a basic braid, but the angles aren't 90° so there are a few differences.

IMPORTANT

To ensure that the finished braid is approximately straight, alternate the wide and narrow ends of the accented and unaccented segments as you add them. If you place the first unaccented segment with the narrower end at the center of the braid, place its accented partner with the wider end at the center. Then place the wider end of the unaccented fabric #2 segment at the center, followed by the narrower end of the accented #2 segment, and so forth.

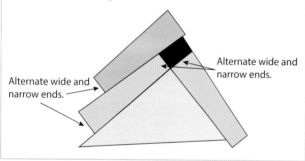

Alternate wide and narrow ends.

Alternate wide and narrow ends.

5. Place a starting triangle on the table in front of you with the 90° corner pointing away from you. When you add the first unaccented segment to the left, do not try to align the ends at the top of the triangle, as the end of the segment probably won't be at the same angle as the top of the triangle. Let just enough of it hang over the edge at the top of the triangle to allow for trimming. Sew a segment to each triangle and press.

6. Align a ruler with the right, unsewn side of the triangle, making sure that it extends past the center end of the segment. Use a rotary cutter to trim the excess fabric from the segment.

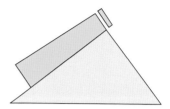

7. Add the first accented segment. If you want the points of the accents to meet, align them carefully at the seamline and pin them. Since the angles are not 90°, they will not align otherwise, nor will they butt. Alternatively, you could just decide to place the seams approximately where you want them and sew. After you have sewn and pressed the segment, trim as in Step 6.

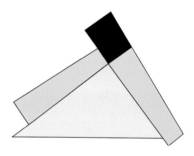

8. Continue adding segments 1–8, and then repeat segments 1–8 to complete each braid. Make 3 braids. Pay attention as you add the segments; if the braid starts to curve to one side, place the wider ends of the segments near the outer edge of that side to nudge the braid into a straighter line.

9. The ending triangles are oversized to allow you to position them with plenty of room at both the tops and the sides of the braids. Add a triangle to the left side first. Place it so the edge of the triangle at the outer edge of the braid finishes about ½″ past the end of the seam attaching the shortest segment on that side of the braid; sew. Press the seam toward the triangle and trim off the excess as you did for the braid segments.

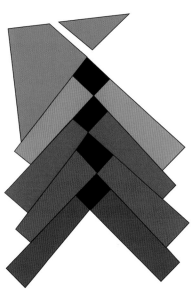

10. Add an ending triangle to the right side, positioning, sewing, and pressing as in Step 9. You should have a few inches of extra ending-triangle fabric at the top of the braid when you finish.

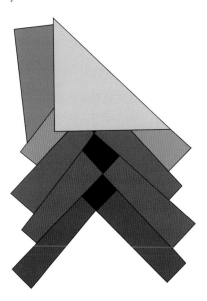

MARKING AND TRIMMING

Read the section Marking and Trimming (page 12).

11. Press the braid, fold it lengthwise down what seems to be the middle of the braid, and lightly press a crease. Lay the braid out flat on a cutting mat. Use the fold line as a reference point to mark the long edge of each braid. This will be determined by the segment that ends closest to the center fold. Mark all 3 braids on both long edges. The 2 long edges of each braid must be parallel, but don't worry if the 3 braids aren't exactly the same width. A variation of up to about 1″ is fine.

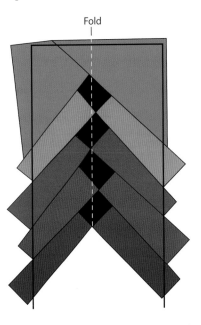

Fold

12. Measure each braid from end to end. Decide on a universal length (see Step 8, page 15) that will accommodate all 3 braids and cut all 3 to that length. The top accent doesn't have to be the same distance from the top on all 3 braids, nor does the starting triangle need to be straight, or even complete. Trim both ends by placing your ruler across the braid at 90° to the lines marked on the braid sides. Find the centers of the long sides by folding each braid in half, matching the ends at their centers. The instructions in Separators (page 16) do not apply here.

Separators, Borders, and Finishing

Read the sections Separators (page 16) and Borders (page 18) .

13. Find the 8 oddly shaped long strips you cut from the braid fabrics. Sew the long sides together, alternating wide and narrow ends, and keeping the fabrics in order 1–8. Press the seams in either direction. (The illustration below shows only 4 of the 8 strips.)

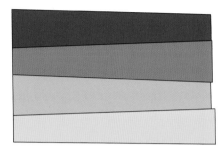

14. Crosscut 4 segments 2¾″ wide from the strip unit made in Step 13. Trim both ends on all 4 segments so they are at a 90° angle to the sides.

15. Sew the 4 segments together into 2 pairs, matching the #8 fabric end of the first segment to the #1 fabric end of the second segment. Then sew a 2¾″ × 11″ piece of ending-triangle fabric to the #8 braid fabric end of each long strip. The separators should be slightly longer than the braids.

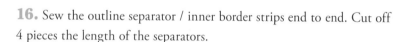

16. Sew the outline separator / inner border strips end to end. Cut off 4 pieces the length of the separators.

17. Sew an outline separator to each side of each separator from Step 15. Trim both separators to the universal length.

18. Sew a separator to the same side of each of 2 braids.

19. Sew the separator edge of 1 of the braids to the third braid. Then sew the braids together to create the quilt top.

20. Add 3 sets of borders.

21. Layer with batting and backing, quilt, and bind.

Parquet

Hot Parquet, 57″ × 74″

The fabric requirements provided below are a bare minimum—you will have enough fabric to complete the quilt, but the more variety you use, the more interesting your quilt will be. The quilt in the photo was made from six or seven fabrics in each of three somewhat analogous colors—red, fuchsia, and orange—with a contrasting accent fabric. Some of my students have successfully made this pattern in a variety of prints with much greater contrast. You need *at least 20 usable inches (20+″) in width* in each fat quarter and *at least 40 usable inches (40+″) in width* if you use yardage for the accents.

Fabric

- **Main fabrics:** 15 fat quarters (This includes 2 fat quarters that will be used in case extra variety or yardage is needed.)

- **Accent triangles:** 3 fat quarters OR ⅝ yard

- **Inner border:** ⅓ yard

- **Outer border:** 2 yards cut lengthwise OR 1¼ yards cut crosswise

- **Backing:** 4½ yards pieced lengthwise OR 3½ yards pieced crosswise

- **Binding:** ⅝ yard

- **Batting:** 61″ × 78″

Cutting

Main Fabrics

- From each of 13 fat quarters, cut 1 strip 8½″ × width (20+″) of fabric. Set aside the 2 shortest leftover pieces.

- From each of the remaining 11 fabrics, also cut 1 strip 6½″ × width of fabric and 1 strip 2½″ × width of fabric. If you don't have enough length to cut a total of 11 strips 2½″, cut the rest from the extra fat quarters or the 2 leftover pieces you set aside earlier.

Accent Triangles

- From 3 fat quarters cut 13 strips 2½″ × width of fabric OR from ⅝ yard of fabric cut 7 strips 2½″ × width of fabric; cut each strip in half at the center fold and discard 1 of the half-strips.

Inner Border

- Cut 6 strips 1½″ × width of fabric.

Outer Border

- From 2 yards of fabric cut 4 strips 5½″ × length of fabric OR from 1¼ yards of fabric cut 7 strips 5½″ × width of fabric.

Construction

SEGMENTS

1. Sew a 2½″ accent strip to each 8½″ main fabric strip. Press the seams toward the main fabrics. Subcut each strip set into 8 segments 2½″, for a total of 104.

If you can't cut 8 from each strip set, cut main fabric segments 2½″ × 8½″ and accent squares 2½″ × 2½″ from your extra fat quarters. Sew them together to obtain 104 segments total. Label these A and set aside.

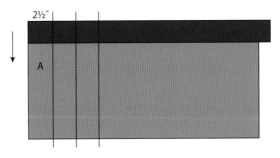

Make 104 A.

2. Randomly select 12 of the A segments, all of different fabrics. Cut off and discard 2″ from the 8½″ end of each piece. Label the leftover pieces B and set aside.

Make 12 B.

3. Randomly select 12 more A segments, all of different fabrics. Cut 6″ off the end of each 8½″ main fabric piece. Label the smaller pieces C and set aside. From 4 of the 6″ pieces you cut off, cut a square 2½″ × 2½″. Discard the rest of the leftovers.

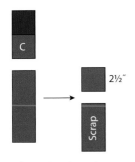

Make 12 C and cut 4 squares from remaining pieces.

4. Select 4 of the C segments. Sew 1 of the squares you cut in Step 3 to each C segment, orienting the pieces as shown and mixing the main fabric combinations. Press the seams toward the single squares. Label them D and set aside.

Make 4 D.

5. Sew a 2½″ main fabric strip to each 6½″ strip. Press the seams toward the larger pieces. Subcut each strip set into 8 segments 2½″. You need 84, so if you can't cut enough from the strip sets, cut 2½″ × 6½″ segments and 2½″ × 2½″ squares from the extra fabric. Sew them together to obtain 84 total. Label these E and set aside.

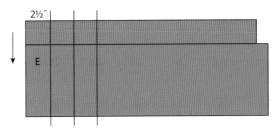

Make 84 E.

6. Select 4 E segments, all of different fabrics. Cut off and discard 2″ of the 6½″ end of each piece. Label the leftover pieces F and set aside.

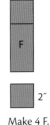

Make 4 F.

UNITS

7. Sew an F segment to the right edge of each of the 4 D units, orienting the pieces as shown and matching the top edges and seams. Press the seams toward the D units.

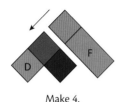

Make 4.

8. Sew a B segment to the left edge of each unit, orienting the pieces as shown and matching the top edges. Match the *seam* in the B segment to the *seamline* near the end of the D unit. Press the seams toward the D units.

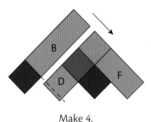

Make 4.

9. Sew an E unit to the left edge of each unit, orienting the pieces as shown and matching both ends. Press the seams toward the E unit. Label the finished units G and set aside to use as the starting units for the columns.

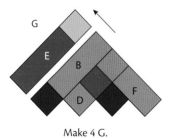

Make 4 G.

10. Select 4 A, 4 B, and 4 C segments. Sew a C segment to the left edge of each B segment, orienting the pieces as shown and matching the *seam* of the B segment to the *seamline* of the C segment. Then sew an A segment to the right edge of each B segment, orienting the pieces as shown and matching the top ends and the seam and seamline as in Step 8. Press all the seams toward the C segments. Label these K and set aside to use later at the tops of the columns.

Make 4 K.

11. Sew a remaining C segment to the right edge of each remaining B segment, orienting the pieces as shown and matching the seam of the B segment to the seamline of the C segment. Press the seams toward the C segments. Label these L and set aside to use later at the tops of the columns.

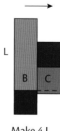

Make 4 L.

12. Sort the rest of the A segments into 2 groups, each with approximately the same number of each main fabric. Do the same for the E segments. Place an E group with each A group. Sew the A and E segments in each group into pairs, orienting the pieces as shown and matching the ends. Make 40 pairs with the longer (A) segments on the left; label them H. Make 36 pairs with the longer (A) segments on the right; label them J. Press the seams toward the shorter segments.

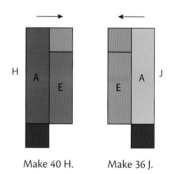

Make 40 H. Make 36 J.

COLUMNS

13. Sort the units into 4 groups, with 1 G, 10 H, 9 J, 1 K, and 1 L unit in each group. Try to distribute the more obtrusive fabrics evenly. If possible, lay out the columns before you begin to sew.

14. Build a column starting with a G unit. Add an H unit to the top right edge, followed by a J unit on the left. Press the seams toward the new additions. Continue adding H units on the right and J units on the left alternately until you have used all 10 H and 9 J units.

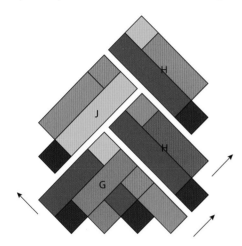

15. Sew 1 K unit to the left top of the column, orienting the pieces as shown and matching the top ends. Press the seam toward the K unit.

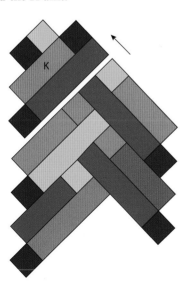

16. Sew 1 L unit to the top right of each column. Match the seamline of the L unit to the first seam at the top of each column. Press the seam toward the L unit.

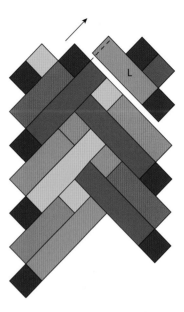

17. Sew 3 more columns in the same way.

TOP, BORDERS, AND FINISHING

Read the section Borders (page 18).

18. Lay out a column on your cutting mat so that the points on the long edge align with a line on the mat. If the column is longer than the mat, align as much as possible and work in sections.

19. Find the points on a long outer edge where the accent seam intersects the seam between the A and E segments. Your *seamline* should go exactly through those points.

20. Lay the ¼″ line of a 24″ ruler on the points you found. The outer edge of the ruler should now be ¼″ past the intersection of the seams. Cut off the segment ends on all 4 sides, sliding the ruler along the sides as needed.

21. To stabilize the bias edges, immediately take the column to your sewing machine and sew a line of stitching around the entire column, about ⅛″ from all the edges.

22. Repeat Steps 18–21 for each column.

23. Lay out the 4 columns. Turn 2 upside down and alternate them with the 2 others. (If you prefer, you can leave them all facing the same direction.)

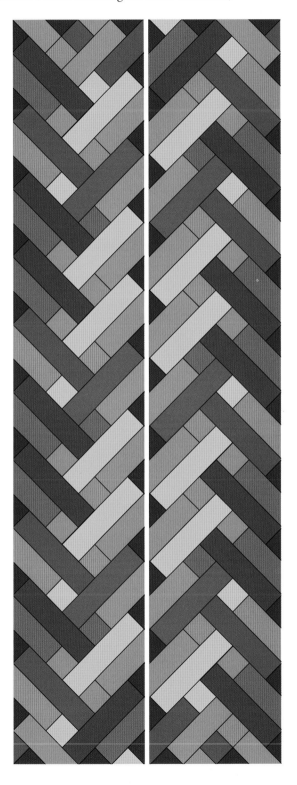

24. Place 2 columns right sides together and pin every intersection. Poke a pin through the top column from back to front at the same seam intersection you found in Step 19. Then poke it through the corresponding point on the second column from front to back. Hold the 2 columns together with your finger, keeping the first pin perpendicular to the fabric while you pin on both sides of it. Remove the first pin. Pin the alternating seams so that they cross at the ¼″ seam allowance.

25. Sew the seam. Go back and check to see that the accent triangle corners meet without spaces or overlapping. Press the seams open.

26. Sew the pairs together in the same way.

27. Add borders.

28. Layer with batting and backing, quilt, and bind.

Cool Parquet, 59″ × 74″ ❖ quilted by Patricia E. Ritter

Triplex

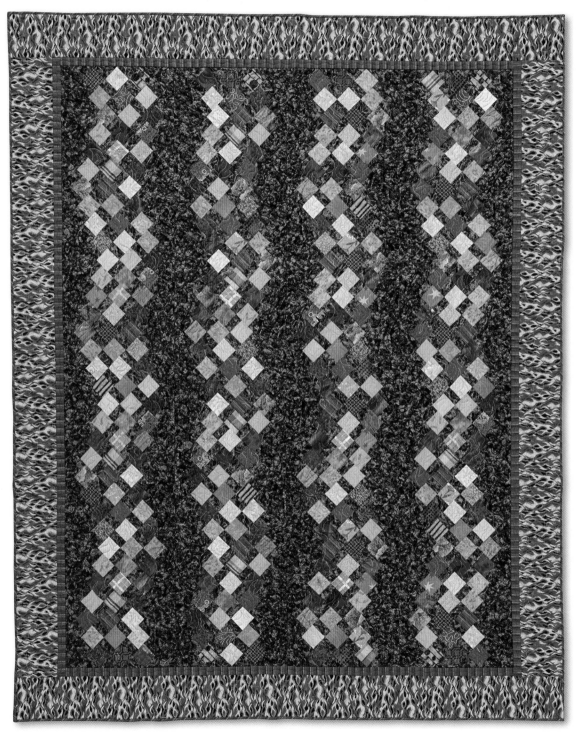

Triplex Fire, 68″ × 82½″

Although the squares that make up the pattern in this quilt are not technically accents, they will be called that throughout the instructions. This version uses three colors for the accents and a fourth color for the background, but the quilt also works well in a more monochromatic palette (page 77). The fabric requirement for the accents is a bare minimum; more variety will make a more interesting quilt. I cut from my stash and used approximately 25 different fabrics, but you could easily use more. You need *at least 20 usable inches (20+″) in width* in each fat quarter and *at least 40 usable inches (40+″) in width* in background yardage.

Fabric

- ❖ Accents: 8 fat quarters OR 9 straight quarters
- ❖ Background: 3⅜ yards nondirectional print or solid
- ❖ Inner border: ⅜ yard
- ❖ Outer border: 2¼ yards cut lengthwise OR 1½ yards cut crosswise
- ❖ Binding: ⅝ yard
- ❖ Backing: 5 yards pieced lengthwise
- ❖ Batting: 72″ × 87″

Cutting

Accents

- ❖ Cut 7 strips 2½″ × width of fat quarter from each fat quarter OR cut 3 strips 2½″ × width of fabric from each straight quarter; then cut each strip in half at the center fold. You will have a few extra strips in either case. If you are cutting from your stash, you will need 51 strips 2½″ × 20+″.

Background

Label each size as you cut.

- ❖ Cut 3 strips 7½″, 2 strips 6½″, 4 strips 5½″, 3 strips 4½″, 2 strips 3½″, 3 strips 2½″, and 18 trips 1½″, all × width of fabric.
- ❖ From 2 strips 7½″, cut 8 squares 7½″ × 7½″; cut each square diagonally twice to yield 32 quarter-square triangles. Label them J and set aside.
- ❖ From 1 strip 5½″, cut 4 squares 5½″ × 5½″; cut each square diagonally once to yield 8 half-square triangles. Label them H and set aside.
- ❖ Cut the remaining strips of all sizes in half at the center fold, making sure that each piece has at least 20″ in width.
- ❖ Cut 1 of the 5½″ half-strips down to 4½″ and place it with the other 4½″ strips.
- ❖ Cut 1 of the 2½″ half-strips down to 1½″ and place it with the other 1½″ strips.

Inner Border

- ❖ Cut 7 strips 1½″ × width of fabric.

Outer Border

- ❖ From 2¼ yards cut 4 strips 5½″ × length of fabric OR from 1½ yards cut 8 strips 5½″ × width of fabric.

Construction

Background is referred to as BG.

SEGMENTS

> **note**
>
> In Steps 1–17, press the seams toward the BG. Try to consistently sew with the BG strips either on the top or bottom as the pieces go through the machine. Keep the ends of the strips even at one end of each set to avoid losing a segment from the set. When cutting strip sets in half, you need at least *10 usable inches* in each half. Label the segments as you go.

1. Select 24 accent strips and 16 BG strips 1½″. Sew the long edges together in the following order to make 8 strip sets: accent, BG, accent, BG, accent.

Make 8 strip sets.

2. Select 2 strip sets from Step 1. Sew a 2½″ BG strip to a long edge of each set. Subcut into 16 segments 2½″. Label them P and set aside.

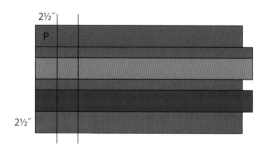

Cut 16 P.

3. Select 2 strip sets from Step 1. Sew a 1½″ BG strip to a long edge of each strip set. Sew a 3½″ BG strip to each remaining long edge. Subcut into 16 segments 2½″. Label them Q and set aside.

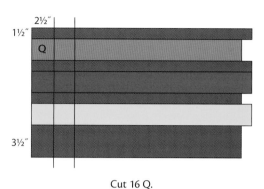

Cut 16 Q.

4. Select 2 strip sets from Step 1. Sew a 4½″ BG strip to a long edge of each strip set. Subcut into 16 segments 2½″. Label them S and set aside.

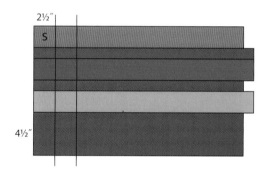

Cut 16 S.

5. You should have 2 strip sets left from Step 1. Cut 1 in half (you need at least 10″ in width) to use now; discard the other half. Also cut in half a 1½″ BG strip and a 7½″ BG strip; you will use the other halves of these later. Sew a 1½″ BG strip to a long edge of each of the strip sets of corresponding length. Sew a 7½″ BG strip to each remaining long edge. Subcut into 12 segments 2½″. Label them V and set aside.

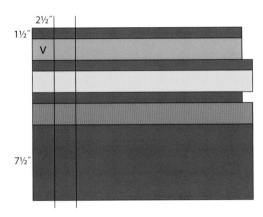

Cut 12 V.

6. Select 18 accent strips 2½″ and 9 BG strips 1½″. Sew the long edges together in the following order to make 9 strip sets: accent, BG, accent.

Make 9 strip sets.

7. Select 2 strip sets from Step 6. Sew a 3½″ BG strip to a long edge of each strip set. Subcut into 16 segments 2½″. Label them M and set aside.

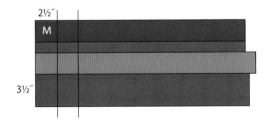

Cut 16 M.

8. Select 2 strip sets from Step 6. Sew a 5½″ BG strip to a long edge of each strip set. Subcut into 16 segments 2½″. Label them R and set aside.

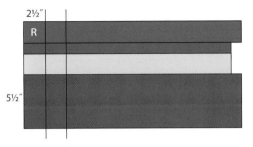

Cut 16 R.

9. Select 3 strip sets from Step 6. Sew a 1½″ BG strip to a long edge of each strip set. Sew a 6½″ BG strip to each of the remaining accent fabric raw edges. Subcut into 24 segments 2½″. Label them U and set aside.

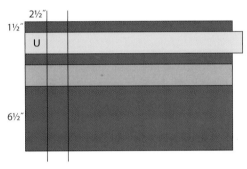

Cut 24 U.

10. Sew a 2½″ BG strip to a long edge of each of the 2 remaining strip sets from Step 6.

Make 2 strip sets.

11. Cut a strip set from Step 10 in half. Set 1 of the half-strip sets aside to use in Step 12. Sew the remaining half-strip of 7½″ BG from Step 5 to the accent fabric edge of the half-strip set. Subcut into 4 segments 2½″. Label them W and set aside.

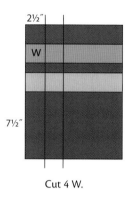

Cut 4 W.

12. Sew a 1½″ BG strip to each remaining accent fabric edge of the 1½ strip sets left from Step 10. Subcut into 12 segments 2½″. Label them N and set aside.

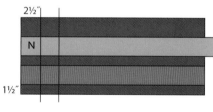

Cut 12 N.

13. Select 5 accent fabric strips and 5 BG strips 4½″. Sew an accent fabric strip to each BG strip, matching the long edges.

Make 5 strip sets.

14. Cut 4 of the strip sets from Step 13 into 32 segments 2½″. Label them K and set aside.

Cut 32 K.

15. Sew a 1½″ BG strip to the remaining accent fabric edge of the last strip set from Step 13. Subcut into 8 segments 2½″. Label them L and set aside.

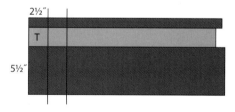

Cut 8 L.

16. Select 3 accent fabric strips, 3 BG strips 5½″, and 3 BG strips 1½″. Sew the long edges together in the following order to make 3 strip sets: 1½″ BG, accent, 5½″ BG. Subcut into 24 segments 2½″. Label them T and set aside.

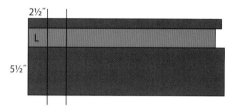

Cut 24 T.

17. Sew the long edge of a 2½″ BG strip to a long edge of an accent fabric strip. Sew a 6½″ BG strip to the other edge of the accent fabric strip. Subcut into 8 segments 2½″. Label them G and set aside.

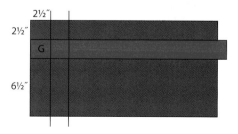

Cut 8 G.

UNITS

> **note**
>
> Be sure to orient all the pieces *exactly* as shown in the illustrations. All the units except A and F are constructed in the same way: by the addition of pieced segments, usually to alternating sides of a starting triangle.

18. Sew the long side of each of the 8 H triangles to the left side of a G segment, matching the centers. Press the seams toward the triangles. Label 4 of them A and set aside.

Make 8 units total. Label 4 of them A.

19. To the remaining 4 units, sew a W segment to the long raw edge of the G segment, matching the centers and 1 seam. Press the seams toward the triangles. Label them F and set aside.

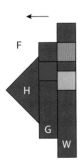

Make 4 F units.

In Steps 20–30, press all the seams away from the triangles each time you add a strip.

20. Place the 32 J triangles on the table in front of you with the long side parallel to the edge of the table; the 2 shorter sides should form an apex pointing away from you. Sew a K segment to the left shorter side of each J triangle, matching the top of the accent square to the top of the triangle. Press. Select 8 pieces to use in Step 21. Label the other 24 units Step 28 and set aside.

Make 32 units total. Select 8 of them for Step 21 and set aside 24 units for Step 28.

21. Sew an L segment to the remaining shorter (right) side of the triangle on each of the selected 8 units, again matching the tops. Label 4 units Step 27 and set aside.

Make 8 units total. Set aside 4 of them for Step 27.

22. Sew an M segment to the left side of each of the remaining 4 units, matching the ends and 1 seam.

23. Sew an N segment to the right side of each of the 4 units, matching the tops and 1 seam.

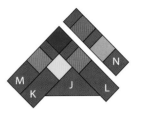

24. Sew a P segment to the left side of each of the 4 units, matching the ends and 2 seams.

25. Sew another N segment to the right side of each of the 4 units, matching the tops and 2 seams.

26. Sew a Q segment to the left side of each of the 4 units, matching the ends and 2 seams. Label these units B and set aside.

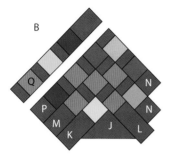

Complete 4 B units.

27. Find the 4 units labeled Step 27. Sew an R segment to the left side of each unit, matching the tops and 1 seam. Then sew an N segment to each right side, matching the tops and 1 seam. Sew an S segment to each left side, matching the ends and 2 seams. Label these units E and set aside.

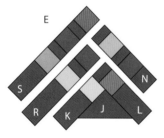

Complete 4 E units.

28. Find the 24 units labeled Step 28. Sew a T segment to the right side of each unit, matching the tops. Label 12 units Step 30 and set aside.

Make 24 units total. Set aside 12 of them for Step 30.

29. Sew an R segment to the left side of each of the remaining 12 units, matching the tops and 1 seam. Then sew a U segment to each right side, matching the tops and 1 seam. Sew an S segment to each left side, matching the ends and 2 seams. Label these units C and set aside.

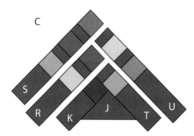

Complete 12 C units.

30. Find the 12 units labeled Step 30. Sew an M segment to the left side of each unit, matching the ends and 1 seam. Then sew a U segment to each right side, matching the tops and 1 seam. Sew a P segment to each left side, matching the ends and 2 seams. Sew a V segment to each right side, matching the tops and 2 seams. Sew a Q segment to each left side, matching the ends and 2 seams. Label these units D and set aside.

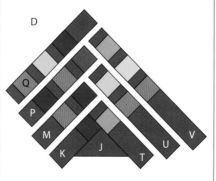

Complete 12 D units.

COLUMNS

31. Divide the various units up into 4 groups so that the more obtrusive fabrics are divided as evenly as possible. You need 1 A, 1 B, 3 C's, 3 D's, 1 E, and 1 F for each column. Lay out each column before you sew it.

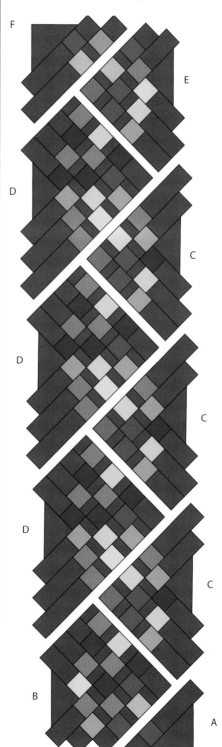

32. Sew a C unit to each of the 4 B units, orienting the pieces as shown and matching the ends and 2 seams. Press the seams toward the C units.

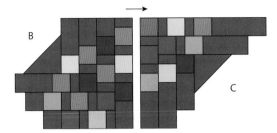

Make 4 BC units.

33. Add an A unit to each BC unit as shown, matching the centers and 1 seam. Press the seams toward the A units. Label the units ABC and set aside.

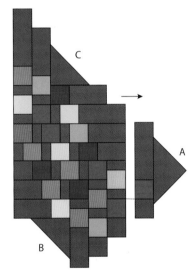

Make 4 ABC units.

34. Sew a D unit to each of the 4 E units, orienting the pieces as shown and matching the ends and 2 seams. Press the seams toward the E units.

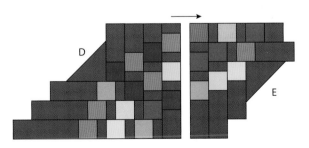

Make 4 DE units.

35. Add an F unit to each DE unit as shown, matching the centers and 2 seams. Press the seams toward the F units. Label the units DEF and set aside.

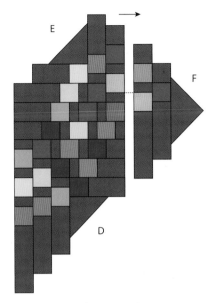

Make 4 DEF units.

36. Sew the remaining C and D units into 8 pairs, orienting the pieces as shown and matching the ends and 2 seams. Press the seams toward the C units.

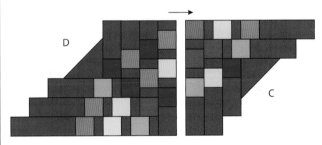

Make 8 CD units.

37. Sew a CD unit to each ABC unit as shown, matching 2 seams and orienting the pieces as shown. Make sure that the *sides of the units continue to stairstep evenly* on both long edges. Press the seams in either direction.

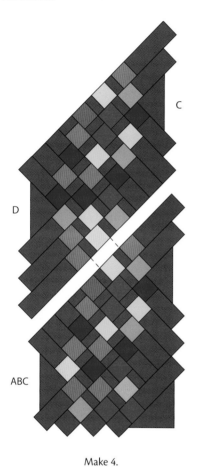

Make 4.

38. Sew a CD unit to each DEF unit as shown, matching 2 seams and orienting the pieces as shown. Make sure that the *sides of the units continue to stairstep evenly* on both long edges. Press the seams in either direction.

Make 4.

39. Sew each unit from Step 37 to a unit from Step 38, matching 2 seams and orienting the pieces as shown. *Check to make sure that you have sewn the long seams correctly by looking at the stairsteps on the sides of the columns.* They should continue evenly in groups of 4 except near the ends, where the groups are 3. Press the seams in either direction.

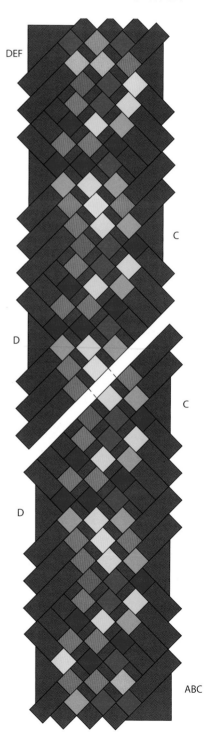

Trimming

40. Lay out a column on a cutting mat, making it as straight as possible by aligning the points on a long edge with a line on the cutting mat.

41. Use a 24″ ruler to measure from the outermost points of the outermost accents as far as possible. You will run out of fabric at the outer edge of the column, where the stairstep edge turns in toward the center. This is about 1½″–1¾″ outside the outermost accent points. The following steps assume that your measurement is 1½″; if your number is different, use that number instead.

42. Lay the ruler on the column with the 1½″ line on the outermost tips of the accent points on one side of the column. Cut off the segment ends and triangle edges, moving the ruler as needed.

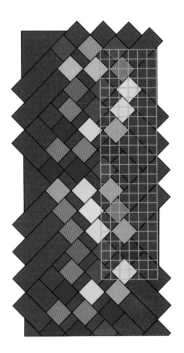

43. Measure from the cut edge to a point 1½″ past the outermost accent points on the uncut long side of the column. This number is the cut width of the column. Use 2 wide rulers or a large square ruler (15″ × 15″) and the cut edge as a reference to trim the opposite side. Trim the second edge, moving the ruler as needed and making sure to measure the same distance from the previously cut edge for every new cut on the opposite edge.

44. Trim both ends of the column by placing the ¼″ line on the 3 accent points at each end of the column. Cut.

45. To stabilize the bias edges, immediately take the column to your sewing machine and sew a line of stitching around the entire column, about ⅛″ from all the edges.

46. Repeat Steps 40–45 for the remaining 3 columns.

BORDERS AND FINISHING

Read the section Borders (page 18).

47. Find the centers of the long edges by folding the column in half. Align a ruler with the row points nearest the fold and mark in the seam allowances on both edges.

48. Sew the columns together by matching the centers and ends, pinning as needed. Then sew the other columns into pairs in the same way.

49. Sew the pairs together to create the quilt top.

50. Add borders.

51. Layer with batting and backing, quilt, and bind.

Baby Blues, 68″ × 82½″

About the Author

As the daughter of a home economics teacher, Jane Hardy Miller learned to sew at an early age. She made her first quilt in 1968, became obsessed with the art in the early 1980s, and spent the next twenty years making all types of quilts. Her discovery of French Braid quilts around 2003 has proven to be a remarkably constant source of inspiration and creativity. She lives in Miami, Florida, and visits the hill country of Texas frequently.

Previous books by author:

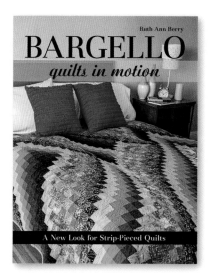

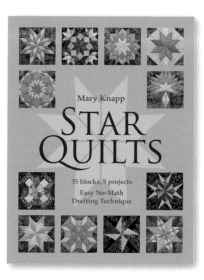